New Japanese Architecture

Revised Edition

by Udo Kultermann

Frederick A. Praeger, Publishers
New York · Washington

BOOKS THAT MATTER

Published in the United States of America in 1960
by Frederick A. Praeger, Inc., Publishers
111 Fourth Avenue, New York, N. Y. 10003
Revised edition, 1967

Copyright in Tübingen, Germany, by Ernst Wasmuth Tübingen, 1960
Library of Congress Catalog Card Number: 60-15601
Printed in Germany

Contents

Foreword

Since this book was first published in 1960, under the title *New Japanese Architecture,* there have been tremendous developments in Japanese architecture. More than almost anywhere else in the world, work done in Japan is on a level with the great architectural achievements of past centuries.

Unlike the first half of the century, when there was a tendency to adopt foreign ideas, as a result of the cultural emancipation that dates from the 1950s, Japanese architecture in the year 1967 has become independent and an inspiration for other parts of the world. While only a few years ago Japanese architects would come to Europe to study and gather information, today it is the West which is looking to modern Japanese architecture with considerable interest and increasing admiration, making a documentation of development since 1960 not only exciting but necessary.

Before 1960, in contrast to the many excellent publications on historical buildings, there were only isolated works on contemporary Japanese architecture, nearly all of which appeared in Japanese publications.

There is, for instance Shinji Koike's *Contemporary Architecture in Japan* (Tokyo 1953) and, in collaboration with Ryuichi Hamaguchi, his *Japan's New Architecture* published in Tokyo in 1956. Hideto Kishida treats only the eclectic results of the adoption of Western forms in his *Japanese Architecture,* first published in Tokyo in 1936. Arthur Drexler, in his splendid volume *Architecture in Japan* (New York 1955), gives only few examples of modern buildings in the appendix, and the book by Iwao Yamawaki, K. Yamakoshi, Masura Katsumi and Torao Saito, *Japanese Houses Today,* deals exclusively with the problem of the individual house, and makes no mention of mass housing, so critically important for Japan.

Recent Japanese books that must be mentioned are the monumental *Contemporary Architecture in the World 1961* (Tokyo 1961) with several contributions on Japan, the books by Kenzo Tange about Katsura and Ise which, although dealing mainly with buildings of the past, nevertheless influence the present situation.

Tange also subsequently dealt with contemporary buildings in Japan, and his own urban proposal *A plan for Tokyo* (Tokyo 1960), had a trailblazing effect. Of importance, also, is the Manifesto *Metabolism 1960 – the Proposals for New Urbanism* (Tokyo 1960), by the young Japanese architects Otaka, Maki, Kikutake and Kurokawa. The books by Noriaka Kurokawa: *Prefabrication and Metabolism* (Tokyo 1960), *House in the future – Metabolism* (Tokyo 1964) and *Urban Design* (Tokyo 1965), so far exist only in Japanese.

The articles by N. Kawazoe 'Modern Japanese architecture confronts Functionalism' (*Zodiac* 1959) and 'The city of the future' (*Zodiac* 1962) give a résumé of this group's ideas in the English language. Guilik Kollandarud wrote about Kenzo Tange in the Norwegian journal *Byggekunst*. Philip Thiel published an analysis of the town hall in Kurashiki by Tange in the *Architectural Review*, January 1961. Heinrich Engel dedicated his large work, *The Japanese House* (Tokyo and Rutland, 1964), to the wooden house, which even today is preferred by the Japanese to all other forms of housing.

Books like J. M. Richards's travelogue *An Architectural Journey through Japan* (London 1963) and the little volume by the Italian Manfredo Tafuri, *L'Architettura Moderna in Giappone* (Bologna 1964), also deal with Japanese architecture.

Important also are the articles by Guenther Nitschke 'The metabolists of Japan' (*Architectural Design,* October 1964) 'Japan's second heroic age' (*Architectural Design,* May 1965) and 'MA – the Japanese sense of place in old and new architecture and planning' (*Architectural Design,* March 1966). Several architectural journals published special issues on Japan, for example *Bauen und Wohnen* 1, *L'architecture d'Aujourd'hui,* and *Architectural Design* 5, 1965.

In this book, which has been extensively revised, work done since 1960 has been incorporated, including a number of buildings by Antonin Raymond, a European working in Japan; it attempts to give an overall view of Japanese architecture since 1945. Japan shows the direction taken by international architecture, and this book is planned to show how the misleadingly called 'International Architecture' has led the way to a new, socially determined vitality and to new regionalism. Architecture must exist by the demands of the people who live in it, and the environmental conditions that give it shape. Contemporary Japanese architecture is the expression of Japan's dual condition, of the ties with what are now recognized as feudal and Imperialist traditions and the expression of the search after new unfamiliar forms of a socially committed imagination.

In my conversations with Japanese architects, much has become clear to me that literature alone could not communicate. The patience and singleness of purpose that I found characteristic of Japanese architects have given me an essential insight into the Japanese character.

To all the architects who so kindly made photographs and other material available, I should like to take this opportunity to extend my sincere thanks. The drawing of the plans was undertaken by Johannes Erdmann, Dipl. Eng., whom I should also like to thank. I am especially obliged to Mr Guenther Wasmuth, who assisted me in planning the book and did everything in his power to make a careful presentation possible.

Leverkusen, April 1967   U. K.   7

I. Fundamentals

In Western countries Japanese architecture is often looked upon today as a model. Social, as well as aesthetic and architectural, reasons have brought about this situation. We are inclined to think that a certain sensibility of taste still plays a part in Japan which it has lost in the West. But this assumption is based upon a fallacy. Admittedly it would appear that in Japan the arts are still closely related to the community, and that manual and machine work stand on an equal footing in producing well-designed objects for the individual. But the dictatorship system of the last few decades and a complex, pluralist, development since 1945 have obstructed a genuine community relationship, so that even in Japan the new social conceptions have had at first to contend with opposition.

The Japanese are characterized by a deep spiritual affinity with nature which stretches far into their past, and this roots them more firmly in their native surroundings than is the case with Europeans. Nature in all her manifestations directs their lives. There is no escape from her, and centuries of experience have brought understanding. Nature, therefore, plays a far more important part in Japan than in Europe or America, and is a continual source of inspiration. The beauty and harmony of the landscape are as much a part of the picture as volcanic eruptions, floods, earthquakes and droughts. The Japanese learnt early to adjust themselves to these natural forces, not by defying them, but by accepting them in their lives.

Like the natural phenomena of the country, its social structure also induced with the passage of centuries a passive attitude in the Japanese. The feudal system imposed upon them a philosophy which for a long time prevented them from playing an active, creative, rôle and inspired a contemplative frame of mind. This outlook was, in particular, identified with the Buddhist religion. Nature was not disturbed. In his arts and technical employments, man did not oppose her, but sought to create a physical and intellectual environment which was linked to the rhythm of nature and to her laws of evolution. In later periods this led to the emergence of a stylized form in the design of house and garden, in literature and flower arrangement, as well as in the social arts. Today this traditional culture is profoundly respected by the younger Japanese, but its application to the present day is firmly rejected. They rightly see in it an escape from reality into a symbolic world of make-believe. It is true that this symbolism embraces everything in its view. The real world, however, remains in every respect out of contact and changed social conditions, which depend upon altered methods of production, are ignored.

Typical examples of this escapism are the tea ceremony and other customs associated with Zen philosophy. Okakura, in his notable writings, still saw Japan and its culture entirely from this angle. Today the view is that Japanese historical architecture is not entirely a product of Zen thinking, and there are also other equally decisive factors which have influenced the newer Japanese architecture. Among them not the least have been technical developments and social sciences spreading from the West. The simplicity and frugality exemplified in the tea ceremony, the poetry radiating from the asymmetrical tea house in the garden, and the sensibility expressed in the use of basic materials, remain the maxims of all aesthetic form, but each period has to rediscover them and adapt them to the social realities of its own day.

Traditional Japanese architecture is fundamentally an architecture of wood. This is explained, on the one hand, by the country's vast resources of timber and, on the other, by the many earthquakes, which make swift rebuilding and a high capacity for resistance essential. Stone was not used until the 19th century. Japanese buildings are principally designed for the hot and humid summer. The essential tasks are to ensure protection against the frequent rains and to provide sufficient ventilation. The skeleton frame system of Japanese traditional construction derives from these requirements, while also affording a measure of safety against earth tremors; but unfortunately, owing to the nature of the material, not against the fires which these so easily cause. The chief feature of the house, because of the rain, was the deep projecting roof, artistically the most important part of the building. The wood was left unpainted, the effect depending upon the absolute purity of the material. The interior was very simply appointed and based on the dimensions of the Tatami mat (about 6 ft. × 3 ft.). Furniture was unknown apart from a few cupboards. The rooms of the dwelling could be used for various purposes and were not specifically allocated for a particular function.

That perfect picture, so often formed in the West, of Japanese ways of building, living and thinking, makes no distinction between the parts played by historical and social factors, and is therefore unrealistic. For the supreme creation of the house was among other things the result of the status of the Japanese craftsman. The proportions and beauty of Japanese timber buildings of the historic periods have endured and, even in technical respects, can often serve as models for certain new standard building plans, but the traditional Japanese house is an expression of a feudal era, which no longer exists.

For this reason it would be unjustifiable to judge the whole of Japanese architecture on the evidence of the late development of the timber house and of the importance of the Tatami mat as a module of measurement in building, regarding this meticulous unimpassioned, perfection as alone typical. The fantastic roof shapes of Japanese temples, gateways and monuments, and the visionary raptures of poetry and sculpture, as well as the many other manifestations of Japanese culture, are much more expressive of a mercurial, exuberant temperament, which for a short time only, during the classic age, maintained a self-imposed discipline and restraint. A clear historical view of Japanese architecture must therefore take both these characteristics into consideration, if it is to give an unbiased picture of Japanese attainments in the art of building.

Moreover, in considering this question, one thing is generally forgotten. The Japanese house in its disciplined clarity and harmony is a reflection of mastery over a primitive, capricious, emotionalism, a fantastic imagination, and a baroque extravagance, which far exceed the most extreme manifestations of European art. This fundamental Asiatic quality in the Japanese, this tendency to extremes, perhaps distinguishes their art more radically than anything else from the more intellectual approach of the European. As in other spheres of the arts in Asia, these extremes were combined in Japan in the same works. As a result they had a vitality of their own, producing an effect which cannot be logically explained. The familiar view of Japanese architecture, the one regarded as typically Japanese, was confined to one aspect of the architecture of Japan. Its supreme expression was considered to be the Villa Katsura near Kyoto in which perfect spatial proportions and contrasting surfaces were blended in an artistic system of exquisite harmony. From the standpoint of the new movement in the West, at the beginning of the present century, from the angle, that is to say, of Le Corbusier, Gropius, Mies van der Rohe and Bruno Taut, admiration for buildings of this kind, for the Japanese modular art and for their reliance on a few essential building elements, is easy to understand. The result of this onesidedness, however, was that everything which did not fit into this idealized picture of a Japanese 'prototype'-modern architecture was rejected as uncharacteristic and un-Japanese. Some people have tried to see Chinese evidence in features which conflicted with the picture, forgetting that everything originating in Japan can be traced back in one form or another to Chinese influence. Others have dismissed them as merely eccentric or extravagant. The same thing occurred in Europe during the long period of opposition to the Baroque, the real merits of which could not be understood by those trained in strict classicism.

Similar extremes can be detected in the historic development of Japanese architecture from earliest times. In prehistoric days they can already be found in succeeding styles of pottery. In the Jomon period (which lasted until about 200 B.C.) copious ornamentation and an abundance of vigorous formal invention were the rule, in contrast to the Yayoi (which followed from about 200 B.C. to 200 A.D.), when plainness and purity of form predominated. The discovery of these cultures appeared at one time so contradictory to the experts that they long supposed that two racial groups were responsible. But more recent anthropological researches have brought proof that they were one and the same. Several prehistorians would like to see in differing symbols marks of distinction between nomadic hunters and settled farmers, while others, especially in older studies, accept that the Jomon civilization was conquered by the Yayoi, because the Yayoi are looked upon as the real ancestors of the Japanese. This explanation corresponds to a long prevalent view that Japanese culture lay in the arts of proportion and orderly arrangement, a prototype culture, so to speak, of a modern Western kind. Everything which did not fit into this simplified conception was explained as a foreign influence. But the two basic traits are complementary, whether they existed isolated, but side by side, or succeeded one another historically, or were in conflict. Both contribute to a complete picture of Japanese culture.

Foreign influences have always been of decisive importance in the formation of Japanese art and culture, and from this there emerges a fundamental fact that only in contact with other, earlier and greater, cultures was it possible for the Japanese spirit to flower. Thus China exercised her influence for more than a thousand years, and was already doing so at the birth of the real historical art of Japan, the Asuka period (552–654). Everything earlier is regarded in Japan as belonging to archaeological times, since no reliable historical sources are available. It is true that the Shintoist forms of building, which were customary before this period, can be reconstructed, since sanctuaries (e. g. the Ise Shrine) are pulled down in each generation and rebuilt to the identical plan. At the beginning of the Asuka period Buddhism spread through Korea to Japan (552), and this naturally had its effect upon architecture. In the forefront of building activities and artistic endeavour were generally the temples, which followed the Chinese style, itself influenced by India. Painting and sculpture similarly reveal Chinese inspiration. When we reflect that Indian Buddhist art is derived partly from Greek models, an unbroken succession of early cultures is apparent, stretching from Egypt, through Greece, Persia, India, China and Korea to Japan. The most important monument of the Asuka period is the still preserved temple group of the Hôryû-ji, dating from the beginning of the 7th century, with its golden hall, pagoda and central gate, which has survived nearly 1500 years and must be the most remarkable architectural work in timber in the world. With its treasures of painting and sculpture, it stands as one of the most impressive monuments to Japanese art of the early period. It is characterized, however, not by a sensitive refinement, but by strength and a vigorous handling of materials.

The subsequent Nara period (645–794) also adopted the art of the Chinese empire, which left its mark in a majestic harvest of superb monuments, like those of the Sui and Tang dynasties. Buddhism had now become the state religion of Japan and guided her arts to new heights. Some historians in consequence have regarded the Nara period as supreme in this sphere. The principal works of this era (the Shôsôin treasure house of 756, the Hokkedo of the Todaiji of 733 and the Yumedono of the Hôryû-ji of 739) are concentrated for the most part in the town of Nara, which gave its name to the period.

The Heian or Kyoto period (794–1185) followed the golden age of Nara. It began with the transference of the capital from Nara to Kyoto. New Buddhist sects grew in influence and the connection with China was temporarily suspended with the withdrawal of the Japanese embassy from that country in 894. Japan was now obliged to preserve and exploit her own sources of inspiration without the constant stimulus of new ideas from China. During the Heian period court life in Kyoto achieved a high degree of luxury and refinement. In architecture the Shinden-Zukuri style emerged in which the house is sited asymmetrically in a garden. Among important buildings of this period are the pagoda of Daigo-ji at Kyoto of 951, the main hall of Joruri-ji at Yamashiro of 1047 and the Phoenix hall at Wji of 1053.

The age of refinement and courtly elegance was succeeded during the Kamakura period (1185–1392) by a strong régime founded on military power, which moved the capital from Kyoto to Kamakura. This was the great era of the Samurai, when new links were established with China. The Zen sect dominated Buddhism, opposing all outward display and preaching – in accordance with the austere standards of the Samurai – intellectual discipline and extreme frugality. The new attitude towards nature excluded all idealism and substituted a practical philosophy. An example of the architecture of this period was provided by the hall of relics of the Engaku-ji at Kamakura, destroyed by an earthquake in 1922, which dated from the end of the 13th century.

The Muromachi period (1392–1573) represented at first a continuation of the Kamakura era, but the austere attitude was modified in the arts, and the refinements of life were revived. The tea ceremony was created, and the tea house became its architectural expression, while its increasing influence upon the art and life of the time is clearly apparent. The golden pavilion of the Rukuonji monastery at Kyoto (circa 1400) is a product of this period, as are the Renga poetry and Nô plays. The Muromachi epoch inclined towards decorative richness, but the tendency was more marked in the short Momoyama period (1573–1615). It was at this time that contact was first made with European civilization, and this probably had a considerable effect. But soon everything coming from the West was suppressed, and a long period of isolation began. Once again the castle and palace architecture with its vigorous painted and carved ornamentation dominated the arts.

In the Edo period (1615–1867), Japan lived for more than two hundred years in total isolation from the West and in complete peace. But in course of time the work of artists declined into a lifeless stylization due to an absence of creative inspiration from abroad and to barriers imposed by social restrictions. In architecture the peak was reached at the beginning of the period with the 17th-century Villa Katsura near Kyoto. Whilst here a harmonious balance of mass and line is achieved, the gate of the Shinto temple at Nikko, completed in 1636, offers an abundance of ornament, baroque in its richness. Thus in this period also the contrasting extremes of Japanese art found expression. It was not until 1868 that isolation was ended and the floodgates of Western influence opened.

These basic characteristics dominated architecture until about 1870. From this point the newer developments encountered an obstacle, which has only been surmounted in recent years. Because of the centuries-long isolation of her life from the West, Japan stood in 1868, technically speaking, at the stage of development of a mediaeval feudal state. A break now occurred for the first time with an architectural tradition ruled exclusively by religion. As the Japanese were completely inexperienced in building with stone and metal, they had first to resort to importing and copying Western buildings in order to keep pace with Europe and America. The new tasks of architecture in the industrial age, however, were not only unfamiliar in Japan, but even in the West only found appropriate solutions after many errors and digressions. So it was that Japan, during this early phase of her modern civilization, in tackling the building problems made necessary by 'emancipation', repeated the mistakes of the West.

The light, traditional, Japanese building methods with wood could not be applied to the construction of railway stations, city office blocks and factories. Architects were, therefore, commissioned from Europe, who used their own materials and methods. At that time people in Japan did not realize that they were also adopting the follies and mistakes of the much admired Western world, and suffered in silence. Thus Ende and Böckmann, architects from Germany, designed the law courts and parliament buildings in Tokyo and influenced a large number of Japanese architects, who zealously imitated them. Similarly, Josiah Conder from England began to teach in Tokyo, and as a result the English Gothic revival was introduced to Japan. Cappelitti from Italy built the military museum in Tokyo, as well as offices, and taught at the high school. He, too, proved a negative influence. A pretentious style emanating from France and the U.S.A. was much in evidence in Yokohama. Most of these architects, and official Japan as well, were caught in the vicious circle of representative 19th-century architecture. At first, therefore, Japan did not benefit in the field of art and architecture from any Western creative inspiration, but assumed the tasteless artificialities of a technical world dominated by the standards of officialdom and social position. It needed the havoc of the great earthquake of 1901 to demonstrate to the Japanese the absurdity of this architecture. They began to appreciate that masonry could be combined with skeleton frame construction, and this may have been the reason why Frank Lloyd Wright, America's still neglected genius, was invited to Japan. Wright brought with him a new conception of design, which was to prove the first important lesson learnt in this country from the West. His Imperial Hotel in Tokyo employed the new frame construction and was the only building in a wide area which withstood a later earthquake.

Gradually the Japanese turned away from the false protagonists of the West, from the official architects of governments, to artists with inspiration. The 'Jugendstil' architects, Otto Wagner, Joseph Maria Olbrich, Henry van der Velde, Josef Hoffmann and Peter Behrens, with whom Frank Lloyd Wright in one of the phases of his work should also be associated, now exercised a strong influence, in which the revitalizing power of the new movement outside the frontiers of Europe is clearly apparent, enabling Japan to find for the first time a fresh creative stimulus in architecture.

The passion of the Japanese for copying, which is often a source of reproach, should perhaps be mentioned here. It must be appreciated that for centuries originality was not considered important in Japan; the manner of execution was what counted and this frequently differed only in small details from what had been done by others. Japan, therefore, knew no succession of styles in the empirical sense, which were so significant in the logical evolution of the West. In the European middle ages the situation was similar. In those days, too, originality of invention was not the significant factor, but the 'anonymously modelled object, which often showed few differences from its predecessors and could, therefore, easily be mistaken for a copy or imitation.

Even nowadays much in Japan is just a variation, either of old traditional buildings or of new major works in the West. Many buildings by younger architects can be traced back, for example, to recent work by Le Corbusier, others to Pier Luigi Nervi (to the UNESCO building in Paris, perhaps, or the sports stadia in Rome), without any attempt at concealment. Others again seize upon the latest phases of architectural development in America, by Mies van der Rohe, Eero Saarinen or Felix Candela. But this is not just a matter of imitating the external shell; in most cases the fundamental conception is appropriated in its entirety and is the cardinal factor in the design.

During the past century we can on the whole speak of an exchange of influences between East and West, in which each side has given and taken. Just as the Japanese at first took from the eclectics, then from 'Jugendstil' and Wright, Le Corbusier, Gropius, and Mies van der Rohe, and latterly from revolutionaries like Candela and Saarinen, so the West has learnt from Japan; for example, Wright and many of the European pioneers from the traditional Japanese house. In 1882, Christopher Dresser, having spent four months in Japan, recommended the use of Japanese models to Europeans in the same way that Winckelmann had recommended the copying of Greek models in the 18th century. In both cases, the detour via a model-culture was considered the return to nature. Dresser had much influence on the Art Nouveau movement which was popular in Europe after 1890. Very recently young Japanese architects have begun to receive tangible appreciation in the West. Kenzo Tange has gained awards both in France and the United States, and young architects from Waseda University have won international prizes at São Paulo. Takamasa Yoshizaka was given a First Prize in an international competition for an African community centre, and the bold designs of Kiyonori Kikutake will no doubt soon be reflected in the West.

From about 1920 Japanese architects began to build in the style of European models, first merely copying, but soon erecting buildings suitable to their particular needs, while using the essential features of the original. Individual Japanese had already taken their cue from Europe in the 19th century, like Kiugo Tatsuno, who in 1896 completed the Bank of Japan and in 1914 the railway station in Tokyo. Such buildings symbolized the first stage in the adoption of Western building forms by the eclectics, who introduced no genuine architectural revival. The second stage began with the early works of architects still active to-day, like Sutemi Horiguchi, Togo Murano and Mamoru Yamada, as well as of Tetsuro Yoshida, who died in 1956. Admittedly a large number of classical-eclectic buildings were still built, like those of Y. Matsumoto, K. Ishimoto, C. Sone, S. Chujo and S. Ito, but the decisive pioneering work was done by the group which took as its models Le Corbusier, Walter Gropius, and also Hans Poelzig, Erich Mendelsohn and Bruno Taut. Frank Lloyd Wright proved influential with the Imperial Hotel in Tokyo, and Antonin Raymond instructed many young Japanese architects in hitherto unfamiliar building-methods. After the general influence on the arts of Art Nouveau, a second source of inspiration entered Japan, the results of which are still detectable nowadays. The basic ideas of Mies van der Rohe and Le Corbusier, which have spread to most countries in the world, led through every kind of opposition to a disciplining of the means of creating form and to more positive possibilities of architecture. Japanese architects recognized the fundamental tendencies in Western architecture and with a sure instinct made both these masters their teachers.

But this architecture of contrasting planes was bound to seem unsuitable for Japan in the long run, even if it had much to give. Owing to the Japanese climate and the need for maximum cross-ventilation, and because of frequent earthquakes, skeleton frame construction was essential. Moreover, architectural forms originating in Europe and arising out of her ascetic, formalist, attitude, were hardly appropriate to Japan, so that developments inevitably followed other lines.

As in many other countries, the years after 1930 brought a formal sedateness, a certain rigidity and stiffness, and artistic activities in general suffered a decline under dictatorships of the period. In Japan imperialist circles gradually gained the upper hand, and this affected the arts and social conditions. The war with China made the position hopeless and many architects were forced to take routine jobs in the massive expansion schemes launched in both Manchuria and China. World War II deprived architecture, which by its nature is completely opposed to all the destructive implications of warfare, of the entire basis for a creative existence. Thus the promising developments of Japanese architecture of the 1920s were cut short before they could bear fruit.

After 1945, because of poverty and lack of materials, no significant buildings appeared at first. The destruction had spread a general artistic lethargy over the country, the occupying powers providing the principal commissions. As in Germany, no genuine building activity started until about 1950, but from this point, mainly after the peace-treaty between America and Japan had been signed in San Francisco in 1951, progress was astonishing. Understandably architects turned again to the achievements of the days before the war with China, that is to say they relearnt the vocabulary of functionalist architecture from the beginning. The old masters of the Japanese modern movement, like Yamada, Horiguchi, Murano, Kume, Yamaguchi, Sakakura and Mayekawa, as well as Antonin Raymond who was working in Japan, fulfilled the important function of intermediaries, supplying an architectural yardstick for the general artistic revival.

Soon, however, the generation which had completed its training since the war began to come forward, and today the scene is dominated by their buildings. The most important names are Kenzo Tange and Takamasa Yoshizaka, Kenji Hirose and Hiroshi Oe, Yoshinobu Ashihara, Motowo Take and Fumihiko Maki and Makoto Masuzawa, Masato Otaka and Kiyonori Kikutake, Noriaki Kurokawa, Sachio Otani and Arata Isozaki. With a few exceptions their names are still almost unknown in the West. Yet their works contain the qualities which may develop into a future Japanese architecture.

More and more young Japanese architects talk, not only of links with the West, but also of the bonds uniting them to Asia, and this is a significant pointer to the way ahead. A new recognition is emerging in structural techniques of the particular 'Japaneseness' of Japan, and this has led to a critical attitude towards Western developments. In concrete frame construction – although often reflecting later work by Le Corbusier – forms have been devised essentially suited to the Japanese climate, which correspond better to their traditions than the functionalist designs of the 1920s. It is characteristic that today not only one side of Japanese tradition, that of the tea house and of the Villa Katsura, is considered important, but also the other, recorded in the majestic temples and towers of the Nara period. The one-sided approach to building, which was a product of a European attitude of mind, has been overcome in Japan, and a complete expression of the innate character and spirit of the people is now sought. That this expression has to a large extent a social basis and is seeking to present, as perhaps hardly anywhere else, an architectural statement for a new society, is in line with the general tendency of our age and, despite many national and geographical differences, offers one more proof of a clear, common goal among creative architects. It is centred in a desire to change men's surroundings and to collaborate in creating an environment which will convey a sense of mankind's interdependence.

II. Problems and Solutions

As in other countries, architecture in Japan is determined not only by the architects, but by the clients, by society in fact, which shapes the physiognomy of its architecture by the way it defines its requirements. In the following pages we shall try to clarify this social basis of architecture with examples of some of the particular problems of building posed in Japan.

In the field of town-planning, like most other countries, Japan has found no new solutions. Towns sprawl without method into the surrounding country. Statutory building controls seldom reveal the enlightened principles of young architects like Otaka, Kikutake and Ito, which are regarded as utopian visions. Kenzo Tange, one of Japan's leading architects, has said: 'Our authorities only recognize the need for reconstruction and clearance after a catastrophe. They see no necessity to prevent the recurrence of catastrophes by a new programme of building.' This comment epitomizes the situation. Although Tokyo has twice been nearly destroyed in the 20th century, no appreciable changes have been made. The great majority of houses are still constructed of wood, which increases the danger of fires in an earthquake, nor is there yet either a comprehensive drainage system or a general gas supply.

In addition, the urban population is increasing rapidly. It is reckoned that the population of Tokyo, 10 million in 1961, will rise by 1975 to 15 million. Drastic remedies must be devised. Regional and urban planning is essential, and this must take into account the living and working conditions of the community as a whole, and the age of existing buildings. It may be relevant to refer here to the plan of Noriaki Kurokawa for the centre of Tokyo, which proposes higher buildings than those customary at present. Dwellings are envisaged which will be built on stages carried on concrete piers, thus increasing living space in a vertical direction. In an island country, like Japan, which has little chance of finding more room, projects of this kind are particularly important. Other plans are concerned with a second possible solution to the problem of living space, the natural opportunity offered by moving 'on to' the sea. Here, too, the new ideas have been confined to the capital, Tokyo. When the president of the Japanese housing association, Kyuro Kano, proposed a satellite town on or in the bay of Tokyo, the younger architects came forward with a series of further suggestions. Kano thought of placing a dike across the bay to form a new land area on the Dutch model. The new town would lie in the eastern half of the demarcated part of the bay. The young architect Masato Otaka goes further in his proposals. He takes the view that there is no point in placing a dike across the bay and enclosing it, and then having to drive concrete piles for the buildings into the solid ground. He, therefore, advocates building the houses individually in the sea, taking Venice as his model, and not Holland. For these projects there are a number of variations, which have already been worked out and could be realized within a measurable space of time. One important advantage of Otaka's over the Kano plan is based on economics; about 50% of the costs of the dike scheme would be saved.

Another young architect, Kiyonori Kikutake, goes one step further still and carries the idea of moving the town on to the sea to its logical conclusion. His proposals include huge floating concrete rafts. Like Otaka, Kikutake advocates high blocks of flats in the new order of city planning, and thinks in terms of mobile waterborne housing units (plate 173). Multi-storey blocks, each with 3,000 inhabitants would hang from these floating concrete rafts, which would have open light wells in the middle. The outside walls of the blocks would, therefore, be surrounded by water, only the inner sides being open to the air. The top surface of the concrete rafts could be used for gardens, community activities, heliports, etc. Submarines would provide direct access to the city from the base of the towers. The significance of this project, in contrast to the dike schemes, is that the housing shortage could be finally solved, since in principle unlimited space can be obtained.

As elsewhere, however, the town planners in Japan are largely administrative officials, while the architects are usually independent private practitioners, and creative ideas and administrative routine seldom go hand in hand. The profession of architecture has never been very highly considered in Japan, a factor which may be linked with the general attitude towards life; all things – according to the nature and religion of the country – are transitory and of small importance, and this philosophy is also applied to building.

The traffic problem remains unsolved as well. The cities still contain many streets in which two cars cannot pass. Roads in urban areas for fast traffic without intersections have not been effective in early experiments. Radical planning measures are urgently needed to cope with the rapidly progressing industrialization of Japan, and if the work is started in time, great economies will be possible. The negative experiences of other countries may be able to teach a lesson here.

For centuries domestic building has been the characteristic expression of Japanese architecture. It has left its mark on other building types, and the most important achievements have been in this field. Since 1945, however, there has been a fundamental change. Today it is not domestic building which plays the principal rôle in the new Japanese architecture, but the great community and administration buildings. The far-reaching social revolution which has occurred in the past fifteen years seems to be expressed in this development. As in hardly any other lands, with the possible exception of Denmark and Finland, many Japanese towns are distinguished by municipal and community buildings of outstanding architectural interest. The sense of mutual dependence of the Japanese, which was for centuries suppressed under the authoritarian régime of the Shogun and Emperor, can now blossom freely. This community spirit is developing a daring new architecture in public buildings, which is still lacking in the individual private home. But the new town halls erected to serve the community are not merely buildings for the present and the future, but also have links with the past, of which they are far more a part than buildings copying the outward forms and decorative features of Japanese tradition. The old Japanese skeleton - frame construction is experiencing a revival thanks to concrete, although based on a different technique, and today, as in the past, offers architects scope for imaginative design.

MUNICIPAL AND PUPLIC ADMINISTRATION BUILDINGS

Since the erection of the city hall at Shimizu in 1954 by Kenzo Tange (plates 2–3), a recognizable building type has emerged, which is regarded as a model for Japanese town halls and which has found its happiest interpretation in Kenzo Tange's building for the Kagawa prefecture at Takamatsu on the island of Shikoku (plates 8–13). Only the competition scheme by Makoto Tanaka for the city hall at Shimonoseki, which in 1952 introduced a new form of town hall to Japan, can be considered as a precedent. Tange's town hall type comprises a flat, low, building of 2 to 4 storeys and a high block of 8 to 10 floors. The low building contains offices for public business, while the high block has offices for those matters in which direct public access is less essential, together with assembly hall, council chamber and public rooms. The arrangement of the auditorium and offices varies according to the size of the town. The meeting halls are sometimes placed at street level, where they can serve as the town's community centre.

An excellent example is provided by the town hall (plates 6–7) and centre of Imabari, in Ehime prefecture, by Kenzo Tange (1959). The conception of a community forum has been put into practice on an impressive scale. The structural design recalls the masterly simplicity of Le Corbusier's handling of concrete, but also Pier Luigi Nervi and Tange's teacher, Kunio Mayekawa. Yet an independent approach is everywhere apparent, brilliant in its interpretation of spatial values and of the needs of a new kind of community.

Another important group of buildings in Japanese post-war architecture is also a city hall by Kenzo Tange, the municipal government centre of Tokyo (plate 1), a rare example of perfect understanding between the client's requirements and the architect's solution. Tange planned a huge tripartite group of buildings, consisting of a large administration building sited transversely, an assembly hall and a high office block; these, however, were never executed. The office building was intended to provide the principal feature of the entire scheme. The administration block is carried upon a sequence of concrete piers extending the full length of the ground storey, which is set back, the horizontal lines of the seven upper floors being strongly emphasized. The recessed windows are protected from the sun by projecting balconies. Tange's town hall in Kurishaki (plates 14–15) represents a new concept as much in the altered relationship between civil servants and the population as in the architectural forms which express this new relationship. This hall, too, was originally to be enlarged by a community centre and is only a fragment of what was intended.

Other architects have also made important contributions to the new order of town halls. Among the most convincing of these are the town centre of Setagaya, a flat-roofed building by Kunio Mayekawa, with a south wall recalling Nervi's UNESCO conference hall (plates 36–37) and the municipal building at Hajima in Gifu prefecture by Junzo Sakakura (plates 20–21), which was built for a town formed from a group of smaller places lying close together. Kenji Imai, in his splendid town hall at Otakimachi, has made a particular point of incorporating the work of sculptors and painters.

The young architects Okuyama, Komiya, Kaji and Fujimoto were responsible for the new city hall at Nagasaki, a noteworthy achievement. It stands close to the sea and plays a considerable part in the urban scene (plates 16–19). The main building and the separate assembly hall are on different levels, which produces a lively 'stepped' effect. The administration building of Shimane prefecture at Matsue is similarly arranged. It was designed by the architectural department of the Ministry of Construction and was erected under the supervision of Shin Yasuda.

The series of municipal buildings by Takeo Sato are equally impressive: the town hall of Niigata, which was part of the complete reconstruction scheme for the town after the fire of 1955; the town halls at Iwakuni (plate 23), Asahikawa, Bunkyo-ku (in Tokyo) and Kokura. Large firms, like the Nikken Architectural Company, have adopted the ideas of Kenzo Tange and built town halls at Sakaide, Seto and Sapporo of high quality. An impressive town hall to the design of Katayama was built in Nara. Kisaburo Ito has built one at Honjo, and Shizuo Ban and Tomoya Masuda another a Minami-ton. Gonkuro Kume erected the city hall at Hamamatsu as early as 1952, Shindo Akashi that of Yamanashi, while Yoshiro Zaniguchi designed the town hall at Takasaki. The list could be extended.

The surprising thing is that many of these buildings have genuine architectural merit and are not, as in most other countries, mere routine jobs by architect-bureaucrats. In addition, it must be stressed that in most cases this characteristic building task represents popular architecture in a practical sense. Administration buildings and council chambers are often used for cultural activities. The town hall is, therefore, conceived as a community centre and frequently includes an auditorium with a stage and projection equipment, and rooms for adult education, libraries and exhibition space. In other instances restaurants, shops and rest rooms are provided.

The general intention is to break down the barriers which separate municipal government and the public, to get rid of bureaucracy, and to create an intellectual centre for the community suited to its size and social structure. One of the strongest arguments of the new architecture that the 'community building' is also a cultural centre is its recognition that the two fundamental tasks are complementary. Building for the community is, in this rightly understood form, always a building for cultural purposes. The building of town halls and community centres has made it possible to pay special attention to cultural requirements. In individual cases the two fields of activity have been combined (Tange's town hall and community centre at Imabari, Mayekawa's centre for the Setagaya district of Tokyo, with an administration building added later – plates 36–37). Since, in many community buildings, stage and film presentations, and lectures and public gatherings are possible, whilst libraries, exhibition galleries, concert halls and sports facilities can be incorporated, there are countless demands, and the use of the building for many purposes is a powerful economic argument.

EDUCATIONAL, CULTURAL AND RECREATIONAL BUILDINGS

A number of new buildings are devoted to educational matters and have no administrative functions, e.g., the centres designed by Hideo Kosaka at Nagoya (plates 34–35), by Fuminaga Kiyota at Tokyo-Nakao (plate 28) and by Togo Murano at Yonaga (plate 29). Also by Togo Murano (in collaboration with Mori) is the cultural centre of the town of Yawata which, in addition to normal community facilities, includes a large auditorium with foyer and a museum of art and applied arts. Shindo Akashi has built the Yamanashi town centre in Kofu. Isao Shibaoka has erected a cultural centre at Tochigi, Kikutake one at Ishibashi, Mayekawa centres at Fukushima (plates 30–33) and Yokohama (plates 74–75), while Kenzo Tange has been responsible for the Peace Centre at Hiroshima (plates 94–97). The latter, which is at the same time a memorial, includes a museum, an assembly hall, a children's library (plates 58–61) and an open meeting place, distinguished by the symbolic Peace Gate.

In general the central feature of these schemes is an assembly hall, about which the other buildings are grouped. At Nagoya the museum, which was completed first, was extended to include a multi-purpose hall. At Fukushima the centre-piece is a concert hall, and at Kanagawa the auditorium and library. Thus in the majority of cases the essential buildings are combined with other functions.

The strong community sense of the Japanese is shown in the many clubs and recreation centres, but these, too, are often combined with buildings for other activities. They may be erected by big firms as holiday homes, like the Matsuhama club house of the Nihon Gas Chemical Industry Co., designed by Yoshinobu Ashihara, in the prefecture of Niigata (plates 82–83), with two wings opening directly on to the sea. Takeo Sato provided a rest centre for the golf club at Ome near Tokyo, and Sutemi Horiguchi designed a building for the Otokiki golf club, which forms part of a hotel, as did Kunio Mayekawa for the NHK Fujimigaoka club at Suginami-Ku, near Tokyo. Sato and Horiguchi used concrete, and Mayekawa wood, but all three fulfilled the requirements imposed. Other typical club houses have been built by Makoto Masuzawa for the Mitsubachi club at Fukuoka, and by Masachika Murata at Aichi (plate 81) and Toyu (plate 80). The Ladies' Centre at Yokohama (1961), by Yoshinobu Ashihara (plates 78–79), satisfies a number of needs, and has a cinema in the basement, shops on the ground and first floors, and a school of dress-making on the second and third storeys. This building is something in the nature of a new building type. The women of Yokohama have been given a central meeting place.

Buildings of architectural interest designed for specific purposes in the cultural field are comparatively rare. There are Togo Murano's Kabuchi theatre at Osaka, which copies the architectural manner of the Momoyama period, being a purely evocative conception therefore, and another in Tokyo by Isoya Yoshida. As an example of a modern Nô-theatre, the building at Nagoya by Jiro Miyaji and Masatavo Suzuki should be mentioned. A few museums have been built, more often than not isolated, in special cases for technical libraries and special craft schools, like the Sogetsu Art Centre in Tokyo by Kenzo

Tange (plates 72–73), entirely devoted to the art of flower arrangement and a product of collaboration with the great master, Teshihara. The museum of modern art at Kamakura by Junzo Sakakura should also be mentioned here, and the Baseball museum by K. Mori, containing everything associated with the game. Another special museum is Minoru Ohta's Noboribetsu Hot Springs museum, which bestrides a river in the form of a bridge, and houses a collection of documents and objects connected with the study of this subject. The small archaeological museum of Kinreizuka, by Hideo Yoshida, Keiji Yoshida, Yasuo Minegeshi and Masao Komiyama, has been built on a very small budget, but it is to be expanded later both as a repository and for holding exhibitions, and will also become a centre for recreation and education. Kikutake designed the museum for Shimane prefecture (plates 70–71), a single-storey building carried on pilotis, lighted entirely from above. The National Museum of Modern Art in Tokyo (plates 68–69), which was built to take the Matsukata collection, stands out as the most impressive museum group. The design stems from Le Corbusier, the execution being entrusted to three architects, who may be described as his most important Japanese pupils: Sakakura, Mayekawa and Yoshizaka. The museum has an ideal site in Ueno Park in Tokyo.

Libraries have usually been built in association with schools and universities, as part of a community project. Outstanding examples are the Kanagawa library (plates 74–75) by Kunio Mayekawa (incorporated in a cultural centre), Tsuda College library at Kodaira by Kenzo Tange (plates 54–55), and one at Seijo university by Makoto Masuzawa (both combined with larger school groups). The public library in Tokyo by Takeshi Takahashi has been designed with a triangular floor plan, which has facilitated book storage and benefited readers. The Children's Library in the Peace Centre at Hiroshima (plates 58–61) breaks new ground both in its form and as a building type. It is planned in the form of a circle, and is designed to the scale and mind of a child.

The project for an aquarium in Ueno Park in Tokyo by Kenzo Tange strives to achieve harmony between architecture and water, while the great scheme by Motowo Take at Nagasaki, on a perfect site with direct access to the sea, will become the largest aquarium in the world.

The place occupied by school buildings in the new architecture of Japan reflects the keen interest in education and intellectual matters of Japanese youth. Of first importance has been the use made by the universities of leading architects, who have prepared comprehensive plans for the universities of Meiji, Seijo and Hosei. Meiji commissioned Sutemi Horiguchi, who grouped the various lecture rooms on a confined site around a garden quadrangle. Recreation and common rooms have had to be provided by balconies and roof gardens, since the inner courtyard is unfavourably placed for the sun.

The buildings for Seijo university by Makoto Masuzawa, which embrace faculty and lecture rooms, are of about the same date. A student's assembly hall, dining room, library and study and staff rooms are being added. The individual class rooms partly open on to semi-circular balconies. Masuzawa has also designed for the same university a sports-hall with a hyperbolic paraboloidal roof.

In 1958 the last building of the comprehensive plan by Hiroshi Oe for Hosei university in Fujimi-cho, Tokyo, was completed. The product of six years' work, this group is certainly among the most important architectural achievements in the field of educational building in the **15** world. Concrete is the chief material, and its possibilities have been exploited to the full, ranging from plain walls and floors in natural concrete to cylindrical shells and hyperbolic paraboloids.

Among other buildings designed for educational purposes, those for Kasei university at Nagasaki, by Takamasa Yoshizaka and Kusuhiko Orii, with their zigzag arrangement of external walls and free, plastic, handling of masses, should be mentioned, and also individual buildings of Kanagawa university by the Ria Group, and the junior college of Eiwa Jagakuin by Hiroshi Oe, which educates girls from Kindergarten to high school level. The assembly hall designed by Hiroshi Oe for the Toyo-Eiwa primary school proposes a huge concrete building with massive walls and projecting roof. An architectural solution in a wooded setting has been achieved by the new building of the University for Economic Studies in Tokyo by the Taisei Construction Company, an extensive reinforced - concrete frame building with uninterrupted balconies round the upper floor.

Primary schools of some distinction have been built by M. Matsumara at Kamiyama, K. Andow in Tokyo, Mano and Sengen, and the Nikken Architectural Firm at Gyosei. In addition, the senior school at Kanazawa by Y. Nagakura, as well as the buildings by Yasumi Yoshitake in Tokyo and Yoka, the school at Osaka by Gonkuro Kume, and the circular senior school at Narashino in Chiba prefecture by the Tokyo Architectural Firm deserve attention. The plan by Yasuo Uchii gives a dynamic form to a school group combined with a church. In its general layout this school group consists of interlocking hexagons, disposed about internal courts, also with six sides.

RELIGIOUS BUILDINGS

As in many other countries, religious building in the main has no community basis today. In consequence, significant work in this field of architecture is rare. We ought perhaps to refer, however, to a few temples by the architects Uno and Akino (Raikoji temple of the Jodo sect, with a saddle-shaped shell roof), Seiichi Shirai (Buddhist temple in Tokyo), Michio Fujioka (Shinjo-Ji temple in Tokyo), Rengo Sekkeisha (meeting room in the Taishakuji temple at Josenji) and the Tokyo Architectural Firm (Kotokusan Seiganji temple at Odawara). In all these buildings present-day materials, like concrete and glass, were exclusively used, and in their shell construction they show the influence of Saarinen and Candela in America. But something of the multi-purpose character of Japanese architecture has even found its way into this religious world, as when the place of worship is also used as a children's day-nursery. The single space principle of the large hall is obviously borrowed, so far as its structural form is concerned, from the public auditorium used for lay purposes, although the absence of seating and of other forms of Western furnishing reveals a clear connection with Japanese tradition. A different concept is represented by the new Izumo shrine by Kikutake, where the religious images of Shintoism are expressed by means of contemporary architecture. Kenzo Tange provided a powerful impact with the cathedral in Tokyo (plates 98–99).

HOSPITALS

The building of hospitals is largely confined to a few architects specializing in this work. The problem in Japan derives in particular from the fact that many hospitals belong to private organizations and only open their doors to a small percentage of the public. The equipment, therefore, varies from the lavishly provided private clinics to the simple homes of smaller communities. The buildings of Mamoru Yamada, whose hospital in Tokyo, erected as long ago as 1937, represents an architectural peak, sets an exemplary standard. His later buildings, like the Social Welfare Hospital (1953) in Tokyo (plates 100–101) and the new University Hospital (1956) at Osaka (plates 102–103), together with his plans for newer and larger hospitals with several wings are distinguished for variety of architectural treatment and for the greatest possible use of light and air.

Another important building is Kisaburo Ito's hospital at Itabashi in Tokyo, which is supported on pilotis, and serves both as the medical school of Nihon University and as a general hospital. In collaboration with other architects, Ito also built the Toranomon hospital, a seven-storey structure grouped about an inner court, to the designs of the late Kaoru Ono. A further instance of a successful combination of general and teaching hospital is the building for Hokkaido University by Togo Rakuto and Minoru Ota, erected between 1953 and 1955.

Large private companies have built Kanto hospital in Tokyo and the Industrial Accident and Insurance Hospital at Kawasaki in Kanagawa Prefecture, which is divided into four blocks and holds about 500 beds. The Central Hospital at Akita in North Japan, by Kiyoshi Ikebe, has 650 beds. The Public School Union has been responsible for building the Central Hospital at Fukuoka with 300 beds (architect: Masao Taguchi), which serves the whole district for out-patients as well as ward cases. A notable small lying-in hospital has been built at Todoroki by Kiyosi Seike (Ishizuka Clinic), a simply organized single-storey concrete block building, whilst Junzo Yoshimura has designed for a smaller area the Kambara Public Hospital in Shizuoka Prefecture, a plain three-storey building, provided at modest cost for four townships in its immediate neighbourhood. Another recent example is that of the Narimasu Mental Hospital erected in a Tokyo suburb by Kiyonori Kikutake (plates 104–105). In this relatively small building, comprising two wings, concrete is used in an almost sculptural manner.

SPORTS BUILDINGS

Sports buildings in Japan are generally combined with other activities, such as municipal community centres, schools or club houses. Thus the Shizuoka convention hall by Kenzo Tange (plates 106–107) was built in the first place for gymnastic meetings, and then adapted for cultural and social occasions. The town sports stadium at Ube, by the Taisei Construction Company, can hold 3,000 people for sports events and some 8,000 for conventions. The sports stadium of the town of Fukui takes its form from the triangular form of the suspended roof. The Tokyo Olympic Games of 1964 were marked by the building of new stadia by Masachika Murata (plates 112–115) and by Kenzo Tange (plates 116–119).

HOTELS, OFFICES AND COMMERCIAL BUILDINGS

In fairly recent years hotel architecture in Japan has received a splendid stimulus from Frank Lloyd Wright's Imperial Hotel, but this notable building has found no real imitators since. The principal hotel architects reflect a Japanese tradition, to which they are all directly linked. Thus in the superb Hasshokan Hotel by Sutemi Horiguchi, with ts many associated buildings, interior and exterior achieve a harmonious unity which has rarely been matched. Tetsuro Okada and Isoya Yoshida have also built hotels deeply rooted in tradition. But those by Iwao Yamawaki at Kinugawa Spa and Kawaji Hot Springs are closer in structural technique to the West, while Masachika Murata's designs for his Kirishima Kogen Hotel and the adjacent mountain lodge are developed entirely from the landscape about them. In the Nikko youth hostel Yoshinobu Ashihara created a building with a marked horizontal emphasis in the hill country near Tokyo. It stands out sharply against a wooded background and at the same time blends with its surroundings by the use of natural stone walls. (plates 86–87). Further excellent hotel buildings were designed by Tange (plates 120–121), Kikutake (plates 122–123) and Akui (plates 124–125). In almost all hotels and other communal buildings, the bath house plays a fundamental part and often occupies a central position. The woodland site of the bath house of a hotel at Yonaga, built by Isao Shibaoka in 1957 (plates 126–127), deserves mention in this respect. In the field of holiday homes the architects of the Rengo Sekkeisha Group and Yoshiro Taniguchi have done impressive work.

Office buildings occupy a large place in the total volume of building, since a great deal of workspace has had to be provided in a short time for Japan's highly industrialized society, but work of architectural quality in this field is comparatively rare. Prestige is still the primary consideration. But in individual schemes a good standard has been reached, as in the buildings for the Japanese railways and, even more, in those for the post office. Particularly distinguished examples of the latter are to be seen in the post offices of Tokyo (1931) and Osaka (1939), both major works of Tetsuro Yoshida. Since World War II Hideo Kosaka has been in charge of postal building. The post office savings bank buildings at Kyoto (plates 128–129) and Nagoya (plates 130–133) are built to his designs, and each is a fine instance of a combination of traditional basic forms with modern materials. A number of city office blocks are by Kunio Mayekawa and the firm of Takenaka Komuten, but these in many cases suffer from a certain rigidity in conception and the use of standardized type plans. Mayekawa's various banks also reveal no new ideas. The Miki building by Hiroshi Oe, and the Chuo-Koran office building by Yoshinobu Ashihara, however, are very striking examples of a successful blend of clients' needs and architectural form. The administration building for the Ogochi reservoir dam at Kitatama-gun near Tokyo – built by Toshiro Yamashita (plates 134–135) in an isolated position – also reflects the sculptural qualities of concrete. Problems created by the latest phase of technology and mass-communication (television studios) have been solved with notable success in buildings by Gonkuro Kume, Fuminaja Kiyota and Toshiro Yamashita. Kenzo Tange proved influential with his two buildings for the Dentsu Company in Osaka (plate 141) and Tokyo. Further office buildings were erected by Kiyoshi Kawasaki in Kobe (plates 136–137) and by Hiwaka and Sakakura in Osaka and Ofuna.

In department stores Japanese architects have anticipated developments, which have today spread from the United States throughout the whole world. The retail trade is concentrated in central shopping areas with cultural and social facilities. Thus large stores not only contain many sales departments, but cinemas and theatres, space for recreation and education, museums, planetaria, railway stations and office accommodation. They are rightly described as town centres and, together with the official social centres, play an important part in community life. The two most prominent store architects in Japan are Togo Murano and Junzo Sakakura, both characterized by their individuality, but united in the task of solving a contemporary problem, although by different means.

INDUSTRIAL BUILDINGS

Industrial building presents a fairly new problem in Japan, where hand crafts were able to maintain their position well into the 20th century. Owing to the pressure of economic requirements, the shortcomings of the West in this field, which were at first so marked, have been overcome with astonishing speed. One of the most interesting buildings of the last few years, erected for the Dainippon Ink Company by Ichiro Ebihara, adds offices, a welfare building and a storehouse to an existing factory. The form of the office block, with its reinforced concrete frame and glass walls, recalls the Fagus works of Gropius, but also shows the influence of more recent American examples. The staff welfare building includes bathrooms, medical facilities, a smoking room, a kitchen, a canteen (which can be used for social events) with a stage, and a roof garden. The roof of the storage building is of concrete shell construction, thus following a trend in recent Western architecture. The decisive factor, however, is once again the multi-purpose character of the accommodation, which expresses a keen sense of cultural and social responsibility. For the roof of his factory at Kamata, near Tokyo, Go Okamoto uses hyperbolic paraboloidal shell construction of reinforced concrete, which reminds us of similar designs by the Spaniard Felix Candela, now living in Mexico, while the factory at Hatano in Kanagawa prefecture by the Ria Group has a zigzag pattern concrete roof, into which skylight windows are inserted. A good example of a power station was built by Junzo Sakakura at Kiso in 1954. Toshiro Yamashita has provided the milk industry with a technically flawless, functionally precise, framework in his dairy at Hoya near Tokyo (plates 144–145) and the Yasui Architectural firm's factory for the Kotobuki-ya Brewery Company at Yamazaki, near Kyoto, sets a standard for the fully automatic plant, its tower-like ventilation shafts making imposing architectural features in the landscape. Taneo Oki and Haruki Miyajima gave the printing works at Lidabashi the form (too cramped perhaps on the inside) of a shell vault, and shell roofs also characterize the building of the Press Company factory at Kawasaki in Kanagawa prefecture by the Ria Group. Yutaro Irie has designed for several textile mills (plates 146–147) a basic building type which provides ample, unobstructed, space and good top-lighting. Kiyoshi Kawasaki built model refineries (plates 148–149) in Kobe and Otsu. The most important post-war industrial building is the printing works at Numazu by Kenzo Tange (plate 142), completed in 1954. Here the clients also required plenty of space, free from obstruction, and the solution is both technically sound and architecturally satisfying. As in the case of factories, wide-span roofs play a fundamental rôle in exhibition and sports buildings, so that such structural considerations often determine the design.

EXHIBITION BUILDINGS

Exhibition buildings are expected to serve, in every respect, as a visible expression of the materials and construction methods used, and **17** to provide a general picture of architectural trends. Thus the West became familiar with Japanese architecture principally through her exhibition buildings; for instance, Sakakura's pavilion at the Paris International Exhibition of 1937, Mayekawa's buildings for the Brussels 'Expo 1958', Horiguchi's work at the Biennale at São Paulo in 1954, Yamawaki's at the New York Trade Fair and Yoshizaka's for the Biennale at Venice. Each of these buildings revealed to foreigners particular aspects of present-day Japanese building, from the harmonious interiors of Horiguchi and Mayekawa, with their respect for tradition, to Yoshizaka's eager acceptance of new materials. For exhibitions in Japan, also, interesting architectural solutions have been found, as in the Machinery Hall by Horiguchi for the Peace Exhibition in Tokyo in the 1920s, the exhibition hall in Kobe (1950) and the International Trade Centre in Tokyo by Masachika Murata (plates 150–155), which was erected in a very short time in 1959, thanks to splendid co-operation between architects and engineers. The features of this large scheme are three halls, the second of which – although based on designs by Pier Luigi Nervi – with its exciting dome (diameter 390 feet), is a splendid tribute to Japanese post-war architecture. Kiyoshi Kawasaki's proposed designs (plates 156-157) for Expo 70, the 1970 World Fair to be held in Osaka, are the expression of ideas appropriate to modern exhibition architecture.

TRANSPORT BUILDINGS

Like roads, transport buildings have not yet been developed in Japan to the same extent as in some other countries. Railway stations are often combined with other functions, including such facilities as department stores, theatres, blocks of offices and planetaria. This is the case with the station buildings by Sakakura, in Tokyo and at Nagoya by the Nikken Architectural Company. Airport buildings have been erected by Fuminaga Kiyota (plates 158–159), Hideo Kosaka, Matsuda and Hirata. Among modern service stations those by Junzo Sakakura at Yokohama deserve particular attention in which a system of mushroom construction is employed on the model of Felix Candela.

DOMESTIC BUILDINGS AND HOUSING SCHEMES

Domestic building was for centuries Japan's principal architectural task, simplicity, rather than display, being the keynote of the last three hundred years. In volume of building housing occupies a middle position, but war devastation has increased its importance. In 1945, however, the situation was catastrophic, although on earlier occasions dwellings have had to be rebuilt, since earthquakes and fires have caused constant destruction. In 1945 there was a shortage of about 4.2 million homes, and it was consequently necessary, as in Europe, to take emergency measures. By 1958 the housing shortage had been reduced by more than a half.

Because domestic buildings in Japan are usually of wood, it is difficult to cope with the problem of a dense population. In addition, the Japanese are almost exclusively accustomed to having their own house with a garden. Since the 1920s there has been a revolutionary trend towards concrete and steel construction, which has been applied, in particular, to the detached private home, and latterly, to multi-storey flats. After the important achievements of Horiguchi and Yoshida of thirty years ago, who tried to transfer what were essentially European

prototypes to Japan, the tendency since the war has been to experiment with the mass-production of separate, single-family, houses (e.g. by Kenji Hirose, Kiyoshi Seike and Gonkuro Kume) and with the building of a few notable individual examples by leading architects (Yoshizaka, Kikutake), in which the medium has been concrete. The activities of Kenji Hirose deserve special mention. Since 1953 he has designed more than thirty types of detached house, all using standard components and suitable for mass-production. The basis of Hirose's system is the steel frame, as is also true of the buildings by Isao Shibaoka and Kiyoshi Seike, Masahiro Shiono and Gorozo Iizuka. This method represents a startling continuation of Japanese tradition and is in complete contrast to the houses of the 1920s, which were founded on a different conception, European in origin, of interpenetrating flat surfaces.

Unfinished concrete has only been used for a short time as a basic material for the detached private home. A conspicuous example is the Villa Coucou by Takamasa Yoshizaka (plate 160), which caused heated discussion among Japanese architects at the time of its completion. Its features are a cavern-like form, with external walls in natural concrete and internal partitions disposed in a novel and lively, but unconventional manner. Other architects like Mizuki Yamada have built houses with concrete frames and shell roofs, Shinichi Horao the Kono house at Takarazuka for the Takenaka Construction Company, and Isao Shibaoka the Inoue house at Ogikubo. Naoyuki Inada, and especially Kiyonori Kikutake, have revealed new ways of using this material. Kikutake's 'sky-house' (plates 162–165), raised high in the air on four piers, may well be regarded as an epoch-making model.

The chief material for domestic building, however, is still wood, in which architects of each generation continue to find new architectural possibilities. Among designs inspired by the traditional values of the Japanese house are many dwellings by Junzo Yoshimura and Makoto Masuzawa, Kiyoshi Seike and Gonkuro Kume, the Rengo Sekkeisha Group, as well as a large number of other Japanese architects. Experimental building with new materials like plastics is only at an elementary stage. By way of examples, the buildings and projects by the architects Sannosuke Inoue and Kyo Tamura should be mentioned in this context.

The small house competition for young architects sponsored by the magazine Shinkenchiku produced interesting results. The decision to limit the size to 65 sq. metres (about 700 sq. feet) proved an excellent means of rationalizing the needs of present-day building. Remarkable changes also emerged in the conception of the house, expressed in a closer relationship between kitchen and dining room and in the transference of the kitchen from the customary north to the pleasanter south side. In this development the emancipation of Japanese women and the consequent sense of equality and co-operation in family life have played their part.

While the detached house still represents the principal share of the total volume of building, communal housing schemes and blocks of flats gain favour very slowly, since this mode of living is unfamiliar to the Japanese. Moreover, it is in most cases too expensive. There are, therefore, few outstanding examples of terrace housing, among the best being the scheme for employees of the Fuji Juko Company at Omiya by Tsutomo Ikuta and terrace houses by T. Miyamoto. Housing schemes at Osaka by Gonkuro Kume, built with municipal support in

954, and at Tobata, by Isao Shibaoka, for workers of the Asahi Glass Company break new ground.

Only since 1956 have high flats become an urgent task for an architect in Japan, although there have been individual examples for several decades, built by private contractors. The Nishinagabori Apartments at Osaka, by the Osaka Architectural Firm, include several types of flat, which vary according to the floor, and the Ichinohashi Apartments comprise two groups of owner-occupied flats on eleven storeys with shops on the ground floors. Kunio Mayekawa and the Mido Group built the noteworthy Harumi Apartments (plates 166–167), in which the social implications of the problem were first recognized, and the cost of which was incorporated in the state financial programme. The Apartments have ten storeys and contain 170 flats of various types. Access corridors and lift stops occur only on every third floor. The flats with-out corridors enjoy good cross-ventilation. The structural plan of the block obviously owes much to the Unité d'Habitation of Le Corbusier, but a form has been devised suited to the particular conditions of Japanese life. The young architect Kiyonori Kikutake has built a 'unité' (plates 168–169) based on similar theories at Yokohama.

As is clear from this example, comprehensive housing schemes are possible through the building of flats for employees of large firms, and are beginning to appear. There are also hostels, like the one for bachelors at Omori, near Tokyo, by Junzo Sakakura, which has individual bedrooms, together with dining rooms, common rooms, bathrooms, etc., and another for employees of the Chiba Kogyo Bank by R. Kitadai. In the same category is the residential building for male staff of Japan Air Lines at Yukagaya, near Tokyo, by the Azusa Architectural Firm, which has a private wing and public rooms.

III. Biographies of Architects

ANTONIN RAYMOND

In the frontline of the architects who founded a new epoch of architecture in Japan stands a non-Japanese, who has nevertheless contributed greatly to our understanding of the Japanese: Antonin Raymond. Born in 1888 in Kladno, Bohemia, Raymond was a student at Prague University. In 1910 he went to America where he worked in the offices of Cass Gilbert, busy at the time with the construction of the Woolworth building in New York. Raymond returned to Europe in 1914, but soon returned to the States, invited to Taliesin by Frank Lloyd Wright. He worked with Frank Lloyd Wright for a further year, and then independently for several years on commissions which included the reconstruction of the Garrick Theatre in New York.

In 1919, Raymond returned to Wright who had just then been commissioned to build the Imperial Hotel in Tokyo. Raymond, involved in the plans for this building, accompanied Frank Lloyd Wright to Tokyo and supervised the work. After its completion he did not return to America but remained in Japan to open his own architectural offices.

Talking to Kenzo Tange, Raymond once recalled how surprised he was on his arrival in Japan, some forty years before, to find that all they were trying to bring to their new architecture was expressed in Japanese farmsteads and Shinto shrines like Ise. Then a farm was a model of integration, quite perfect and possibly without parallel anywhere else in the world. It grew out of the soil like a tree, natural and inevitable, developed totally convincingly from its proper function. All structural parts could be clearly recognized from the exterior, the structure itself was both ornament and end. All the materials were natural, selected and worked by true craftsmen. Everything about it and in it was direct, simple, functional and economical. The people, their clothes, tools, pots and pans, paintings and gardens all had a marvellous unity of purpose. They had a clarity which had developed naturally over the centuries and contained, like everything else in nature, the principles of the absolute... These were and must remain timeless, invariable and unalterable, and must be a guide in attempts to create new beauty in architectural design.

Early buildings by Raymond – a school in Tokyo (1922); his own house in Tokyo (1923), the Russian and French embassies in Tokyo (1929 and 1930), are the *incunabula* of architectural revival in Japan.

After World War II Raymond was given the opportunity to execute buildings in America, China, Indonesia and India, as well as a large number in Japan. There is for example the Reader's Digest building in Tokyo, completed in 1949 and the most important post-war building in all Japan. There are several churches, the Gumma Music Centre in Takasaki (plates 76–77), a large hall in steel and concrete, and finally the University of Nagoya (plates 50–51) of which he directed the planning and

execution. There are numerous other buildings besides: his own new house combined with his office in Tokyo, the American embassy in the Japanese capital (1952), a bank in Nagoya of the same year, the library of Mitika University in Tokyo as well as the Fuji Country Club (both 1959).

TOGO MURANO

Born in Kyusyu in 1891, Togo Murano is one of the pioneers of the new Japanese architecture. After studying at Waseda University, he passed his examinations in 1919. A further period of training in the office of Setu Watanabe at Osaka lasted until 1929, when he opened his own office in the same city. Murano has been largely associated with the construction of big department stores and as early as 1935 had been concerned with the design of the Sogoh store at Osaka. In this extremely important architectural problem of modern society he has tried from the beginning to provide more than a series of rooms exclusively devoted to the display and sale of goods, and to introduce other amenities for the public. In recent years the department store, and even more the shopping centre, besides its concentration of sales space, poses problems which were recognized and studied by Murano comparatively early. The store is logically interpreted by him as a building with solid external walls and an interior for the most part artificially lighted. The surface of the exterior is broken up into decorated panels. The form of the building, therefore, appears as the decorative cladding of a functional framework, somewhat like the designs of Edward D. Stone in the U.S.A. This architecture of ornamental patterns can easily lead to stylization. In addition to his large stores, Sogoh at Osaka, Takashima-Ya in Tokyo, the Yomiuri Hall for Sogoh in Tokyo and the Maruei Store at Nagoya, Murano has also built the Grand Theatre and Fujikawa Art Gallery at Osaka, the town hall at Yonaga (plate 29) and the town centre at Yawata, as well as a number of restaurants and houses.

MAMORU YAMADA

Like Murano, Mamoru Yamada is one of the oldest exponents of modern architecture in Japan, which in its revolutionary work of the twenties and thirties effectively counteracted eclectic influences from the West. Born in 1894, Mamoru Yamada studied at Tokyo University and is today one of the most distinguished hospital architects. His early work reflects features of Jugendstil, which was studied with close attention in Japan in the 1920s. His Telegraph Office in Tokyo (built in 1925), in the marked vertical emphasis of the window arrangement, the curved roofs and massive cubic forms, stands half-way between Jugendstil and Expressionism. But the Teishin hospital of 1937 is a fine piece of architecture, which still compares favourably with later hospitals by Yamada and other architects. This 261-bed hospital has a reinforced concrete frame and is faced with porcelain tiles. It comprises two wings and represents a justifiable translation of Le Corbusier to Japan. In 1953 Yamada built the Social Welfare Hospital in Tokyo plates 100–101); it is distinguished from earlier work by the Y-shaped ground plan and increased size of windows. Continuous balconies envelop the building, which is open to the light on every side. At the point of intersection of the three wings is a glass-fronted observation tower, accessible to patients by a spiral ramp. Yamada built a further hospital for the University and City of Osaka (plates 102–103) between 1954 and 1956. It is substantially larger, but the design principles of the Social Welfare Hospital in Tokyo are preserved. Here, too, continuous balconies are provided and, so far as is possible, the external walls consist of windows, the balcony projections serving as sun breaks. In 1956 Yamada designed a large 600-bed hospital, in which four wings extend from a central entrance-block. In the same year Yamada prepared a plan, for an administration building for the Nagasawa Filtration plant of Tokyo waterworks.

TETSURO YOSHIDA

Tetsuro Yoshida forms a link between Japanese and Western architecture. He was born in 1894 and studied at Tokyo University, later holding a professorship at the Nippon University. In 1931/32 he made a journey to Europe, where he met the German architects, Hugo Häring and Ludwig Hilbersheimer, who encouraged him to write a book which would explain the lessons of Japanese historical architecture to the West. The result was *The Japanese House*, a magnificent work published by Ernst Wasmuth in 1935. Seventeen years later there followed from the same publishers *Japanese Architecture,* a continuation and expansion of the earlier book, and in 1957 his last volume, *The Japanese Garden*. These books caused a considerable stir in Europe and America, because of contemporary tendencies towards simplicity, clarity and standardization, for which the logical form and construction of the Japanese house served as a model. But Yoshida has also contributed major buildings to Japan's architectural revival. Surprisingly, the writer who interpreted Japanese tradition came under the spell of Western influences, as can be seen in his early buildings, like the Post Office at Kyoto (1922), the Telegraph Office at Kyoto (1926), the town hall of Beppu (1928) and domestic work of the period, which were all dressed in the heavy neo-classical clothes worn in Europe at the turn of the century. Nowadays these buildings look stiff and mechanical. Yoshida's really creative development as an architect began with the General Post Office in Tokyo, completed in 1931, altough this change was foreshadowed in an interesting, and largely unknown, industrial building of 1930, which introduced the curved glazed wall. The magnificent corner block of the General Post Office in Tokyo, which appeared a year later, has a reinforced concrete frame and is faced with porcelain tiles. Another impressive structure is the G.P.O. at Osaka, which dates from 1939. As well as in these major buildings, which were influenced by the rectangular architecture of Europe, by 'De Stijl' from Holland, by the Bauhaus and by Le Corbusier, Western inspiration is apparent in the detached private homes erected by Yoshida in Tokyo during 1936 and 1937. Since the war he has been responsible for very few buildings, one of them being a branch bank at Niigata (1951), of which the brick façade shows signs of a return to classicism. Apart from several competition designs, for example, the Foreign Ministry and City Hall in Tokyo, Yoshida now devoted himself entirely to his writings, for a serious illness kept him away from practical work. He died in 1956.

GONKURO KUME

Gonkuro Kume belongs to a section of the profession whose ideas were moulded by a European training and who have consequently tried to translate the results of the new Western architecture to Japan. Born in 1895, he took diplomas in 1928 at the Technical High School at Stuttgart, and in 1929 in London. On his return from Europe he was chiefly engaged in publicly financed housing schemes, a new problem for Japan, but of great importance to the country. A noteworthy example was the scheme of two-storey terrace houses built in Yokohama in 1953. Each block has a reinforced concrete frame and eight dwellings, with large balconies facing the south. Outside stairs lead to the first floor. In 1954 came the housing scheme at Osaka – also publicly financed – which comprises three-storey terrace houses forming a self-contained neighbourhood with a school, children's playgrounds and green spaces. The dwellings, like those of the Yokohama scheme, are arranged according to traditional Japanese internal dimensions. The character of the interior is therefore determined by the Tatami mat. The traditional Japanese way of living answers surprisingly well the needs of the industrial workers of the country and provides an essential opposition to the meaningless adoption of American and European forms and furnishings. In addition to further detached private houses in Tokyo, Kume built in 1952 the massive group of Hamamatsu City Hall. The building is supported upon concrete pilotis and adds distinction to the townscape with its cubic, sharply contrasting, masses and its observation tower.

SUTEMI HORIGUCHI

With his contemporaries, Yamada, Yoshida and Kume, Horiguchi is one of the founders of the new Japanese architecture. Born in 1895, he attended the Imperial University of Tokyo, where he completed his studies in 1920, founding shortly afterwards in the secession movement the first modern union of architects in Japan. Co-founders of this movement, the Bunriha Kenchiku-Kai, were Ishimoto and Takizawa. After Horiguchi had built a machinery hall for the International Peace Exhibition in Tokyo in 1922, he spent two years travelling in Europe visiting the Bauhaus and meeting the leading German and Dutch architects. One result of this journeys was his book, *Modern Dutch Architecture*. He had been particularly impressed by the architects associated with the Bauhaus, 'De Stijl' and 'Wendingen', and this influence was echoed in the buildings which he erected after his return to Japan.

In 1928 appeared the chief work of his early period, the building for the meteorological station on the island of Oshima. Two years later his Yoshikawa House was completed, in 1934 the Okada House, the Nakanishi House in 1936 and the Wasasa House in 1939. The race course at Torida dates from 1936. Since 1945 there have been educational buildings for the Meiji University, the Hasshokan Hotel at Nagoya and the Otokiki golf club house, which is in the garden of the Hasshokan Hotel and, with its uncompromising angularity, offers an **21** interesting contrast to the surrounding parkland. The Japanese pavilion for the Quadriennale at São Paulo was built by Horiguchi. His aim is to continue the 'frame' architecture of Japanese tradition with modern materials, steel, glass and concrete. He has thus tried to bring the East and West together and Western rectangular architecture has seemed to him an appropriate vehicle for this purpose. Although, even in his most recent work, traces of 'De Stijl' and of Walter Gropius can be detected, Horiguchi's style is unmistakably Japanese. Occasionally the exterior of some of his buildings of the 1930 period appear too self-consciously functional, but the interior is always characterized by the Japanese sense of harmony, a quality also seen in the work of his maturity. It is true that among his buildings are a few in which the Tatami mat and the use of wood are abandoned, like the Iwanami House at Bunkyo-Ku, Tokyo. On the other hand are structures steeped in Japanese tradition, like the Hasshokan Hotel at Nagoya, which in its sensitive handling of internal space and variety of detail reflects the spirit which guided an older Japan. Besides his architectural practice, Horiguchi has always been active as a writer. Since his early volume on modern Dutch architecture, there have appeared studies by him of the Shoin and Sukya styles, and in 1955 *Architectural Beauty in Japan,* as well as books on tea houses and the Villa Katsura. Since 1949 he has been teaching as a professor at the Meiji University.

TAKEO SATO

Born in 1889, Takeo Sato went to Waseda University, where he studied acoustics, and early in his career he was called in by other architects as technical consultant on acoustical questions. His work as a painter, a parallel activity to his architecture, shows its influence in the treatment of details in certain buildings. He has written three volumes of essays on architecture under the title *Windows*. As an architect, he owes his reputation above all to his town halls, which have been built at Niigata, Asahikawa, Kokura, Iwakuni and in the borough of Bunkyo-Ku, Tokyo. He has exploited new building materials, but frequently in a rather mechanical manner. Sato's architecture is logical and disciplined. It is transparent and clear, often so much so indeed that one is tempted to wish that a little confusion might mar the preciseness of his work.

One of his more important works is the town hall of Iwakuni in Yamaguchi prefecture, in which concrete is treated in the style of similar powerful sculptural effects. In the International Cultural Centre at Nagasaki, in which the five upper floors are divided into five vertical panels of equal size, the ordered symmetry appears somewhat oppressive. The separate building of the assembly hall, however, offers some relief. While Sato used for the Ome Golf Club, near Tokyo, plain concrete construction to contrast with the hilly landscape, his houses, such as the K. house in Tokyo (1949), exemplify an oddly incongruous blend of Japanese tradition and Western living habits. One of Sato's more recent buildings is the rest centre for employees of a firm at Hakone in Kanagawa prefecture. The concrete frame structure of one wing incorporates living and recreation rooms and sleeping accommodation, while the smaller wing with baths has solid load-bearing walls of natural stone. With this building Sato has created a social centre which, both by the nature of the purpose it serves and in the architectural form which it partly derives from the landscape, presents an effective meeting place for a small community.

MASACHIKA MURATA

Masachika Murata belongs to the middle generation of contemporary Japanese architects. Born in 1903, he grew up as a member of a prominent family of the Ise district, which had close connections with the Imperial court. Murata showed early an interest in the applied arts, which it was his intention to follow, when he attended the Art School in Tokyo. While at first his chief interest was painting, he soon turned to architecture. He became a pupil of the architect Shinichiro Okada, in whose office he worked after finishing his studies at Tokyo Art School. Here he collaborated in preparing plans for the Meiji Life Insurance building, on which Okada was engaged. Later he was made a member of the commission charged with supervising the construction of the Imperial Museum. Murata then went to Paris, where, without any direct participation in architectural studies, he proved himself an acute observer of developments in Europe. Returning home, he found Japan at war with China, and the prevailing Imperialist outlook of the time left him, like so many others of his generation, with no opportunities except to work in Manchuria and Haian with large town-planning firms. His first building after the war, an office block at Yokohama, reveals a rather stiff formalism, but the logic and clarity of his later works are already detectable. His subsequent activities have been chiefly directed towards community buildings, sports centres, club houses and hotels. His Country Club at Aichi (plate 81), with its loosely grouped layout on an uneven site, is a delightful composition; the Oyamadai club building, Tokyo, a two-storey reinforced concrete frame structure, has a light and often open exterior and a well organized internal plan; the two hotels at Kirishima – built with the simplest materials in an isolated position in the Japanese National Park – has an air of friendly seclusion; and the swimming stadium at Sendagaya, Tokyo (plates 112–115), offers an imposing interpretation of this building type. In Hall No. 2 of his International Trade Centre in Tokyo (plates 150–155), Murata and engineer Yoshikatsu Tsuboi have used Pier Luigi Nervi as their model in spanning a wide area unobstructed by supporting piers.

JUNZO SAKAKURA

Junzo Sakakura was born in 1904 and has long been rated as the chief exponent of the Japanese architectural revival. In his work was found for the first time the long sought synthesis of Japanese tradition and the achievements of the international avant-garde. Finishing his studies in the art department of Tokyo University in 1927, he decided to abandon the applied arts for architecture. With this in mind, he went in 1929 to study in Paris, where he spent eight years in the atelier of Le Corbusier, whose influence upon him and upon the more recent architectural developments in Japan has been of paramount importance. His first important work dates from his Paris years, the Japanese Pavilion at the 1937 International Exhibition. This, however, was not only the first major commission of the young architect, but for Europeans the first visible sign of the new Japanese architecture. Sited on a wooded hill, the building with its elegant ramps and walks and sensitive arrangement of open and closed spaces, presents a striking picture of the new Japan. This remarkable early work has only been equalled in Sakakura's subsequent development by the Museum of Modern Art at Kamakura (1952). In the meantime he had been working as a prominent member of a nationalist architectural union and had been active in Manchuria. After 1945 he was at first offered few opportunities for building, and was principally occupied as a furniture designer. There then followed a number of large projects, department stores with various public amenities in Tokyo, and private houses, although these have been more a response to commercial needs. Other recent works, like the Omori bachelors' hostel in Tokyo, derive from analyses of specific building requirements and tend to use synthetic materials in a strictly technical way. The recently completed Hajime town hall in Gifu prefecture (plates 20–21), which reflects Le Corbusier's later work, and the administration building of the Japanese silk industry in Yokohama (plate 140) display a new spirit. With Mayekawa and Yoshizaka, Sakakura was one of the architects of the Museum of Modern Art in Tokyo by Le Corbusier (plates 68–69).

YOSHIRO TANIGUCHI

Yoshiro Taniguchi, who was born in Honshu in 1904, must be regarded as one of the most widely known and, in the best sense, popular architects in Japan, whose work can by no means be described as avant-gardiste. Conservative would be a better term. Taniguchi studied at the Imperial University in Tokyo, where he took his diploma in 1928. Until 1931 he worked as a lecturer and in 1943, after much travelling, was elected to a professorship, which he still holds. Taniguchi's practice includes, in addition to domestic work, educational buildings, such as the important group for the Keio University. He has also built a large cement factory with all its associated buildings at Chichibu. At Karuizawa Taniguchi has erected a number of week-end houses and by disposing small buildings in converging rows has succeeded in creating a sense of community on a modest budget. The interiors of these holiday homes, in their lovely rural setting, are particularly attractive. Taniguchi, also known for his writing, has made a name for himself as a designer of tombs, monuments and memorials which are all exquisite in themselves and suited to their surroundings.

KUNIO MAYEKAWA

Kunio Mayekawa, one of the great figures of Japanese architecture, has had an inspiring influence in general on new building in Japan in his capacity as President of the MIDO Group, which he founded. Like Walter Gropius, Mayekawa, who was born in 1905, has formed a team of young architects who by joint endeavour are working to find new solutions to architectural problems. Like so many of his contemporaries, Mayekawa studied at the University of Tokyo. Soon after his graduation in 1928, he went to Paris and continued his studies with Le Corbusier. Here a small group was formed who, instinctively recognizing the importance of Le Corbusier's work for Japan, took the European master's working methods and artistic approach as their model. After two years' work in Paris, Mayekawa returned home and entered the office of Antonin Raymond. In 1935 he began to practise on his own after he had already figured prominently in competitions, in which he had tried to counteract the pompous mock-architecture of the Imperialist régime (Hinomoto Hall 1936, Showa Steel Works 1937 and Dairen Town Hall 1938). But war with China made creative work impossible. Like other architects, Mayekawa went to Manchuria and Shanghai. Important stages in his career after 1945 have been marked by his factory-produced houses of 1946 ('Premos'), the Nihon Sogo Bank building of 1952, a structure too technical and functional for modern tastes,

the administration building of Okayama prefecture, the Concert Hall and Library at Yokohama of 1954 (plates 74–75), which exhibits the power of contrast in handling internal space, the Cultural Centre in Fukushima of 1954 (plates 30–33), an example of plastic treatment of mass, the Harumi flats in Tokyo of 1959 (plates 166–167), which makes a notable contribution to Japanese housing architecture, and the masterly Community Centre of Setagaya in Tokyo of 1957 (plates 36–37), an exercise in new structural effects with concrete echoing Nervi. Part of the latter recalls in its construction the dais wall of the conference hall of the UNESCO building in Paris, and the hall at Imabari by Kenzo Tange of about the same date. In all these buildings Mayekawa has tried to use concrete in a manner appropriate to the material and in the process has discovered new artistic possibilities. Besides these principal works he has built a large number of houses, administration buildings (e. g. the San-ei Trading Company's offices at Naka-ku, Nagoya), community buildings like the Fujimigaoka club house at Suginami-ku, Tokyo, a traditional timber structure interpreted in a modern manner, and exhibition buildings, such as the Japanese Pavilion at the Brussels International Exhibition of 1958, which like the building by Junzo Sakakura of 1937 introduced the contemporary arts of Japan to the Western world. In these two exhibition buildings, separated by over twenty years, can be clearly seen the changed pattern of development.

Whilst Junzo Sakakura still regarded Le Corbusier as his only guide, Mayekawa has sought to express his country's traditions and the forces linking Japanese culture to the aspirations of the Far East. Mayekawa's work reflects the evolution of Japan's new architecture in all its aspects. With Sakakura and Yoshizaka he has shared the task of carrying out Le Corbusier's design for the Museum of Modern Art in Tokyo (plates 68–69). Opposite this building, in Ueno Park is the Memorial Hall by Kunio Mayekawa.

JUNZO YOSHIMURA

Junzo Yoshimura, one of the few Japanese architects who is as well known in the U.S.A. as in Japan, has had opportunities, like Minoru Yamasaki, for building in both countries. Yoshimura's work is principally devoted to house design. Born in 1908, he studied at Tokyo Art School, where he also took a keen interest in Japanese architectural history, e.g., in tea houses at Kyoto. He took his diploma in 1931, and then worked in the office of Antonin Raymond. Yoshimura gained experience on many buildings designed by Raymond and later worked for some time in the latter's New York office. This established his association with the U.S.A., which is marked by his exhibition house at the New York Museum of Modern Art in 1954. A little later he designed another building in America, a hotel in mountain country at Suffern, N.Y., which was built in collaboration with the American interior designer, Lenore Schwartz. But Yoshimura's principal activities after World War II lay in Japan, where he was elected to a professorship at Tokyo College of Art. From this period date many of his domestic works, the Nagia House (1951), Higashiyama House (1953), Aritomi House (1953) and others in recent years at Sendagaya and Senzoku. In addition to these houses, he has carried out other commissions, such as the small hospital at Kambara in Shizuoka prefecture, the beach house at Morito Sea Shore in Kanagawa prefecture and the textile mill at Meiwa in 1952.

MOTOWO TAKE

As professor at Waseda University, Motowo Take exercises a strong influence today on young Japanese architects. Although he is more important as a teacher than a practising architect, his few buildings set a high standard. Take was born at Nagasaki and studied at Waseda University, subsequently entering the office of Kikuji Ishimoto. Before World War II he was working for this firm in Shanghai. His most significant buildings, however, date from after 1952, like the Community Centre at Sendai, which includes a large assembly hall with a foyer and exhibition space and which – although carried on supports – still preserves the Western conception of a structure of flat surfaces, in the manner adopted by Japanese architects in the 1920s. In the Sports Hall at Sendai, completed in 1952, he tried to bring out more strongly the plastic qualities of the building's mass. In the infants' school at Michiru (1955), Take used a light skeleton frame of delightful elegance, which recalls Japanese tradition in a new context. In his design for a Sports Hall for Waseda University he offers a variant of the forceful architectural ideas of Nowicki and Candela, an oval interior roofed by a hyperbolic paraboloid. Take's chief work is the Aquarium at Nagasaki, finished in 1959, which has been built as the centre-piece of a projected vast aquarium group. After future extensions, which include a pool for whales, and social and recreation facilities, this will be the largest and, in its equipment, the best aquarium in the world. The present completed three-storey building has a reinforced concrete frame and walls of local stone. The handling of the imposing elements which constitute the building and the masterly effects of light and shade point clearly to later works by Le Corbusier, whose Indian buildings display a similar power and monumentality.

ISAO SHIBAOKA

Isao Shibaoka, born in 1911, studied architecture at the University of Tokyo and worked in various offices before he opened his own in 1949. Since this date he has been engaged in housing and flat designing, both as part of the state building programme and on behalf of private firms. This work started with a scheme for employees of the Yonaga plant of the Nohon Pulp Manufacturing Co., and with rented flats on the island of Hokkaido. A year later (1953) there followed housing for glass workers of the Asahi Company at Makiyama. These schemes were expanded to include public bath houses. In 1956 Shibaoka designed state-financed housing for Fukuoka prefecture and also projects for housing societies and private firms. These comprehensive undertakings have been extremely important, because they have entailed town-planning in a complete sense, although Shibaoka has not often had the opportunity to develop imaginative designs. He has also built detached houses, office blocks, hospitals, the cultural centre of Tochigi prefecture, with meeting hall, museum and library, clubs and his own house (with office) in Tokyo, as well as the masterly bath house of an hotel in Yonaga (plates 126–127).

HIDEO KOSAKA

Besides private architects, larger organizations have also had a decisive influence on the new Japanese architecture. Especially noteworthy in this connection have been the buildings of Japanese Railways and of the Post Office. For the postal buildings of the last decade the architect largely responsible has been Hideo Kosaka, who has been a member of the architectural department of the Ministry of Posts since 1937 and chief architect since 1954. Kosaka was born in 1912 and studied at the University of Tokyo, where he took his diploma in 1935. He spent a short period in Matsuda's office (until 1936), before joining the architectural staff of the Ministry the next year. Kosaka's buildings are distinguished by clarity and elegance. In almost every case a reinforced concrete frame is the fundamental feature, the design of the exterior being based on the right angle. This is already apparent in his Nurses' School of Teishin Hospital, Tokyo, built in 1950, which has a rather mechanical appearance none the less. Among other works are the Life Insurance Offices at Sendai and the airport building in Tokyo. His best early work is the Post Office Savings Bank at Kyoto (plates 128–129), a long building set in an old Japanese garden. In addition to the department store at Komatsu and postal buildings at Sapporo and Hiroshima, there are three major works of 1959 and 1960, the Cultural Centre of Aichi prefecture at Nagoya (plates 34–35), which consists of a large assembly hall and many adjoining rooms adapted from a museum completed some years ago, the Post Office Savings Bank at Nagoya (plates 130–133) and the Ministry of Foreign Affairs in Tokyo. All three, in their basic form, are related to the earlier Post, Office Savings Bank at Kyoto. The Foreign Ministry, finished in 1960, is the first government building in Japan conceived in the modern manner, and it marks an important step in the process of surmounting the barriers dividing the government and the people.

TSUTOMU IKOTA

Tsutomu Ikota was born in Hokkaido in 1912 and studied at Tokyo University, where he took his diploma in 1939. Until 1944 he was engaged in various projects of the Japanese government. In 1951 he went to the U.S.A. and taught as a visiting professor at the Universities of Raleigh and Oregon. On his return he became a professor at Tokyo University. He has translated various books by Lewis Mumford and Le Corbusier into Japanese. His architectural practice has been largely confined to domestic work and housing, including detached and terrace houses in Tokyo, Yokohama and Ashikaga. In 1956 came further terrace houses for employees of the Fuji Juko Works at Omiya. These are technically important for Japan and also for their use of concrete, because they introduce a new way of living, which has become essential owing to changed sociological conditions.

KENZO TANGE

In Kenzo Tange's work is crystallized the revival of Japanese architecture through the inspiration of tradition. His buildings, which have become known during recent years in Europe and America, indicate the lines of development which Japanese architecture is likely to follow in the future. Kenzo Tange, born in 1913, first studied at the University of Tokyo from 1935 to 1938, returning to the same school for a further period of work from 1942 to 1945. After gaining his diploma, he entered Kunio Mayekawa's office. During his student days, he took part in three competitions and won three first prizes, but none of these designs was carried out. The first of his own buildings, among them the Exhibition Gallery at Kobe, date from 1950. On the other hand his aquarium project for Ueno Park in Tokyo remains unexecuted. Since 1953 his efforts have been directed to finding constructive solutions to contemporary problems, especially in the design of buildings serving the community. Here we should mention his series of town halls, e.g., Shimizu built in 1954 (plates 2–3), Kurayoshi in 1956 (plates 4–5), the imposing group of Tokyo City Hall in 1957 (plate 1), the Kagawa prefecture buildings at Takamatsu in 1958 (plates 8–13), and Imabari, Tange's birthplace, in the same year (plates 6–7) and the town hall at Kurashiki in 1960 (plates 14–15). In these buildings Tange is following a new path, both architecturally by making appropriate use of traditional forms, and in a social sense, by lowering the longstanding barriers between government and nation. Since the town hall of Shimizu, and especially since the Kagawa prefecture building, there has come into existence in Japan a new building type for local administrative purposes. This embodies, for the various functions of government, a combination of high and low structures on Kenzo Tange's model. Since to Tange architecture is not a separate matter, but always seen in its social relationship, he has become a leading participant in Japan's most important building tasks. Other notable instances of his creative output are the Peace Centre at Hiroshima (plates 94–97), with its splendid children's library (plates 58–61), the assembly halls at Matsuyama (plates 38–39) and Shizuoka (plates 106–107), both typical examples of his dynamic talent for design, the library for Tsuda College in Tokyo (plates 54–55), the printing plant at Numazu (plate 142), the Memorial Hall at Ichonomiya (plates 88–91) and the school of the Art of Flower Arrangement in Tokyo (plates 72–73). All these are centres for the new community life and majestic in their conception of this rôle. In many cases, indeed, they have been influenced by Le Corbusier, whose handling of natural concrete has been an inspiration to Tange. But, apart from his debt to the West, there is apparent in Tange's work an obvious awareness of his own creative powers, and this is expressed less as a Japanese variant of the International Style, as in his realization of another side to his personality, which has deep Asiatic roots. Tange is today a professor at Tokyo University and exercises a strong influence on the younger generation. And, as has been said, he is also known abroad: in 1959/60 he lectured at the Massachusetts Institute of Technology at Cambridge, U.S.A. With his spectacular cathedral (plates 88–89) and the Sports Stadia for the 1964 Tokyo Olympics (plates 116–119), his genius for construction is beginning to affect the West.

HIROSHI OE

Hiroshi Oe deserves mention as one of the most significant architects of schools and educational buildings. Born in 1913, he studied at the University of Tokyo and is today a professor at Hosei University. Since his Graduate School for the latter, built in 1953, an impressive five-storey building supported on stilts, with glass walls, he has been extensively engaged on the Japanese Ministry of Education. In 1958, by his completion of the scheme for Hosei University. Oe had created one of the most interesting educational buildings in existence – and not only in Japan. The chief material is concrete in various forms (reinforced concrete frame and cylindrical shells), mostly exploited with the object of spanning large areas without intermediate supports. Hiroshi Oe has also designed offices, like the Miki building in Tokyo, houses, and schools, of which the primary school of Toyoeiwa-Jagakuin, arranged round an inner court, and the junior college of the same girls' school are outstanding. In a project for an associated sports hall, Oe comes close to Le Corbusier in his handling of concrete.

TAKAMASA YOSHIZAKA

Takamasa Yoshizaka was born in Tokyo in 1917, and spent most of his childhood in Europe, where his father was a diplomat. His basic architectural training was acquired at Waseda University in Tokyo between 1935 and 1941, but the impression gained in his early European days had a profound influence upon him. Finishing his studies in 1941, he remained for a few years to work in the research centre of Waseda University before going to Paris in 1950, where he spent three years in Le Corbusier's atelier. Thus the latter's influence on the training of Japanese architects has continued into the younger generation. In 1956 Yoshizaka was given the chance to build the Japanese Pavilion at the Biennale in Venice, a simple concrete structure with smooth, undecorated, external walls. Before this, and since, he has designed houses, which have aroused widespread interest among architects, because of the imaginative way he has handled brick and concrete like sculpture. In particular, the Villa Coucou of 1957 (plate 160) has been much discussed for its expressions of uninhibited fantasy and its highly original application of synthetic materials, still unfamiliar in Japan. The first large building by Yoshizaka is the teaching block for Kaisei University at Nagasaki, which was completed in 1958 in collaboration with Kusuhiko Orii. The building stands on a sloping site by the Bay of Nagasaki. All the classrooms face the south and give a zigzag effect to the whole layout, a theme which is taken up by the slightly protruding staircase tower. Another group of lecture rooms was built by Yoshizaka for Meisei University at Osaka in 1958. In the summer of 1959 his design won an international competition for a cultural centre at Leopoldville, in the former Belgian Congo. With Sakakura and Mayekawa, Yoshizaka supervised the erection of the Museum of Modern Art in Tokyo (plates 68–69), designed by Le Corbusier. Today a professor at Waseda University, he is also prominent as a writer (books on housing, Le Corbusier and *Form and Environment,* and as the translator into Japanese of volumes on the Modulor.

YOSHINOBU ASHIHARA

Yoshinobu Ashihara belongs to the generation of Japanese architects, whose first buildings have only appeared since World War II. He was born in Tokyo in 1918 and studied architecture at the University of Tokyo, where he took his diploma in 1942. He was then drafted into the Japanese Navy and worked as an engineer during hostilities. In 1946 he won third prize in a town-planning competition, and in the same year entered Junzo Sakakura's office, where he was employed until 1947. At the age of 29 he started his own practice, and about this time his first building took shape, a small health centre at Yawata, completed in 1949. Ashihara went to the U.S.A. in 1952 as a Fulbright scholar, studying at Yale and Harvard Universities. After receiving his Master's degree at Harvard, he worked for a year in Marcel Breuer's office, at the end of which he travelled in Europe with the aid of a further grant, this time from the Rockefeller Foundation. In 1954 he returned home, where he erected a large number of buildings in a short time. Besides houses and interior design, his most important works have been the seven-storey Chuo-Koran building in Tokyo and a centre for a women's organization in Yokohama (plates 78–79), both noteworthy for their straightforward, logical structure, and flexible interior plan made possible by a reinforced concrete frame. Also significant is the employees' club for the Nihon Gas Chemical Industry at

Matsuhama in Niigata prefecture (plates 82–83). Recently completed works include the Municipal Hospital at Yokohama, a youth hostel at Nikko (plates 86–87), an eleven-storey hotel, a gymnasium and a three-storey office building. Ashihara relies upon simplicity and clarity of form. His choice of teachers (Sakakura, Breuer) is no accident therefore, since both, in principle, aim at a similar clearness and harmony. For Ashihara concrete is almost always the chief material, and in his plain rectangular style he understands how to give it the character of a new and unembellished monumentality.

KISABURO ITO
Kisaburo Ito, born in 1921, is today considered to be one of the leading architects specializing in hospital design. His first major building was the Central Social Insurance Hospital in Tokyo, followed by the large scheme for Tokyo University Hospital and the Bokuto hospital. Ito's chief work must be considered to be the Itabashi Hospital for Nihon University, Tokyo, which included clinics, laboratories, study and lecture rooms, library and technical and recreational facilities. A reinforced concrete skeleton frame is used. Among other works by Ito are town halls (e.g., Honjyo and the administration building for Saitama prefecture), the municipal sports stadium at Kesenuma, as well as hotels and offices.

KENJI HIROSE
Kenji Hirose has exercised an important influence on Japanese architecture. This is explained by his concentration on a particular theme, the steel house, of which he stands as the most significant pioneer in Japan. Hirose was born at Kamakura in 1922 and gained his diploma at the Technical High School of Musashi. In 1951 he founded his own firm, and since 1953 has been engaged in a scientific study of the construction of houses with a steel frame, a system which has produced some outstanding solutions in Europe and the United States in recent years. In Japan, however, it has been slow to find acceptance owing to the limitations of her industrial production and other circumstances in Japanese life. In 1953 Hirose therefore built the first house of his planned mass-produced series – SH 1 (Steel House No. 1) – as an experiment for himself. Since then, and especially since 1955, there have followed in quick succession projects and buildings, which all depend upon the principle of mass-production and can be erected with prefabricated components. Moreover, in 1955, 1956 and 1957 a smaller number of houses were also developed with reinforced concrete frames. But Hirose believes above all in his steel houses, and he has performed a valuable service in making clear that steel frame construction can be justified as a continuation of Japanese tradition just as much as modern Japanese timber houses. In this respect his work has been of great educational value.

MINORU OTA
Like Yamada and Kisaburo, Minoru Ota is rated among the more important hospital architects. He was born in 1923, studied at the University of Tokyo and took his diploma there in 1944. Until 1948 he continued to work at the same university, but since that date he has been Professor of Architecture and Town Planning at Hokkaido University. He has translated Siegfried Giedion's book *Space, Time and Architecture* into Japanese. Among his chief works is Hokkaido University

Hospital, built to the plans of Togo Rakuto, which was completed between 1953 and 1955. The Hot Springs Museum at Noboribetsu Spa in Hokkaido was erected in 1957 in the form of a bridge spanning a river. It derives its characteristic form from a concrete arch, which also makes possible a large internal hall. In addition, Ota designed the Clark Memorial Hall for students of Hokkaido University, and has been occupied with town-planning schemes for Sapporo and Kushiro.

MAKOTO MASUZAWA
Makoto Masuzawa belongs to that generation of Japanese architects, who were not influenced in the first place by the great Europeans, but by Japanese architects of the period in between. Masuzawa has himself mentioned the names of Kenzo Tange and Kunio Mayekawa in this connection. He was born in 1926, and after finishing his studies at the Architectural School of Tokyo University joined the Kashima-guni Construction Firm, and then, like Kunio Mayekawa and Junzo Yoshimura before World War II, entered the office of Antonin Raymond. During his stay with Raymond, who consulted him in working out his own ideas, Masuzawa built his first buildings, like the Hara House of 1954, his own house and the Fugetsudo Coffee Shop, all at the age of twenty-eight. These early buildings already exhibited his superb handling of wood, which is exploited with sympathy and ingenuity. In 1956 he started his own practice and soon received his first larger commissions, among them a library/bookstore for Seijo University. Masuzawa solved his problem by dividing it into a glass fronted structure and a solid concrete building for book storage with no natural lighting. The design owes something to Kenzo Tange's Tsuda College building finished in 1954. It has been followed by further extensions to Seijo University, so that by March 1958 completed buildings in reinforced concrete construction included the students' hall, refectory, library, lecture rooms and staff accommodation. The Arts Department is placed on the ground floor with the Faculty of Economics above. Masuzawa used a new structural system for the Sports Stadium of the same university, which is roofed with a concrete shell in the form of a hyperbolic paraboloid. He has also done domestic work, e.g., the T House (1958), K House (1959), Ito House and F House in Hatsudai, as well as a club at Fukuoka. His evolution from the strict forms of the Raymond school to a fresh and imaginative conception of design is easy to trace.

METABOLISM
In 1960, Kenzo Tange's plan for the expansion of Tokyo introduced a new phase of urban planning to the world. After working on the preliminary models at Harvard University, Tange proposed a linear city, lying across the sea between Tokyo and Yokohama. This plan created a new relationship between housing, working, recreational activities and traffic.

Also in 1960, a small publication appeared in Tokyo, *Metabolism 1960 – the Proposals for New Urbanism*. It was the first communication from a group of young architects who, like Kenzo Tange, were working toward the reorganization of the total environment. Metabolism (from the Greek μεταβολή which not only means alteration and variation but also revolution and cyclic transformation) became the metaphor for goals that could only be attained by reaching out beyond what had until then seemed feasible and necessary, far beyond what had until then been seen as the valid aim of architecture. The name also indicated that in questions of future cities not only architects but sociologists, critics, biologists, politicians, engineers and many other professional groups had a part to play. The editors ended the first page of their book with these words: 'In future, others will come to join us. Others again will leave us, and thus the metabolic process will apply also within the membership of our group.'

What are the goals of these Metabolists, who first discussed their projects at the International Design Congress in Tokyo in the Spring of 1960? According to what principles do the architects Kikutake, Kurokawa, Otaka and Maki and the critic Kawazoe, joined in 1964 by Kenzo Tange and Arata Isozaki, work?

Their premise is that the human community is a living perpetuum, a continuous biological process, which does not allow for the application of rigid, schematic principles. This, however, is not to say that the most sophisticated technical aids should not be employed to create an order in which men can live in accordance with their ideas and emotions.

Another criterion common to the members of this group is that they, as architects, never tackle buildings or evolve principles in isolation but always in connection with the city-structure as a whole. All separate activities must evolve from this basis. Town-planning has proved basic and fundamental to all architectural work of our time. No-one has recognized this more clearly than the young Japanese architects. To them, town-planning and architecture have become synonymous, one is unthinkable without the other. Dynamic street architecture emphasizes the architecture of the individual buildings which form its components, and both belong to the organism of the metabolist city.

The metabolist future-orientated desire to create cities for a coming mass-society does not mean breaking with tradition. Paradoxically, it means the very opposite. With the increasing concern for future social development, there came a growing awareness of Japan's architectural past – the temples of Nara and Kyoto, or the ancient large-scale Japanese buildings, whether Shintoist or Buddhist. Thus, past, present and future are on the same plane. Only when the future is squarely faced can the past be fully understood. This statement is reversible and just as true: only men living on the heritage of their cultural traditions are in a position to work for the future.

Like the young European architects, the young Japanese, considerably encouraged by teachers like Kenzo Tange and Uzo Nishiyama, have recognized that rigid planning, overall-planning in the old sense, is no longer possible. They saw that flexibility must play a central part and that the laws of change have to be taken into account. Conditions for working both in architectural and urban terms could be no better than they are in Japan. The trends are latent in the Japanese tradition. Günther Nitschke wrote: 'In Japan, nature strives to lead the eye from the buildings, from all that is static, from the house itself and from the city and its installations on to the changing scene where all is flux and transformation.' The use of the architectural forms of the past for the plans of the future is entirely consistent with a creative attitude. It testifies to an essentially contemporary awareness and the willingness to fulfil the obligations with which we have been charged. The present cannot stand in isolation, it is forever bound by the influences, that is to say the rediscoveries of past creative traditions, and

has the task of carrying these forward to new and unknown spheres of the future. Present, past and future are indivisible.

MASATO OTAKA AND FUMIHIKO MAKI

Masato Otaka, born in 1923, is the oldest founder-member of the Metabolist group. He studied architecture at Tokyo University. Subsequently he worked for several years in Kunio Mayekawa's office, where he concentrated on mass-housing. He was largely responsible for the designs of the Harumi apartments (completed by the Mayekawa office in 1956). This was the first important pioneering-work in Japanese domestic architecture. Otaka, still with Mayekawa, also did the principal work for the Cultural Centre at Fukushima.

Although the influence of Le Corbusier's Unité d'Habitation is still evident in the Harumi Apartments, the design approach of these large buildings is already modified in terms of the Japanese situation. Later, Otaka chiefly occupied himself with urban development.

Even before 1960, he proposed an alternative plan for the expansion of Tokyo into Tokyo Bay. Unlike Kyuro Kano, whose plan involved draining the bay with the help of dikes, Otaka realized that it would be better to create artificial islands on which to house people. His final plan proposed a linear city, stretching alongside the coast between Tokyo and Yokohama, with an industrial area facing the sea. The residential districts are facing the coast and recreational and entertainment centres lie between the separate residential strands.

Fumihiko Maki belongs with Kikutake and Kurokawa to the original Metabolist core. He, more than anyone, established the link with the Western world. Born in 1928, he first studied in Tokyo and then in America, where he took his diploma at Cranbrook Academy. He worked in the firms of such architects as Skidmore, Owings and Merrill, José Luis Sert and later with Kenzo Tange. For a time, he also was assistant Professor of Architecture at Washington University. His practical and theoretical work, done in collaboration with Masato Otaka, was of fundamental importance for Japanese architecture. Both architects have attracted attention with individual buildings.

In 1964, after leaving Mayekawa's office, Otaka built the Assembly Hall for the Union of Japanese Seamen in Tokyo. In 1960 Maki built the Toyoda lecture hall for the University of Nagoya, a long concrete building which was added to the other University buildings and also contributed to the redevelopment of the town's eastern sector. In 1967, several buildings for Rissho University were completed.

Metabolism 1960 published Maki's and Otaka's article 'Towards Group Form' – much reprinted since – which states the fundamental architectural theories and principles shared by the Metabolists. Faced with the actual conditions in our large cities, Maki and Otaka do not feel that architecture in the traditional sense could ever come to terms with the problem.

In their view most of our cities are hopelessly chaotic or drearily stereotyped in accordance with the schemes of a few dogmatists. Cities lack individuality not only in the separate elements that make them work, but in their whole character, which is monotonous. There is no flexibility, no elasticity with regard to social and economic changes, nor is there any appropriate visual means of coming to terms with the gigantic road-systems and aerial perspectives.

These two young architects question the architectural developments of the last thousands of years in their proposals. No longer is the single **27** building of main importance, however perfect – pyramid, Parthenon, cathedral or Seagram building; these architects aim to destroy the concept of such essentially fixed, static elements. 'Group Form' is determined by several buildings and their relationship to each other. It goes much further than similar forms of the past: Horyu-ji in Nara, the Piazza del San Marco in Venice or even the new urbanism of Chandigarh and Brasilia.

The goal of Group Form is not the architectural group as we have inherited it, made up out of fixed, static edifices, but a new spatial entity, architecturally planned, in which the structure is in a state of balance with its separate elements. For Otaka and Maki, the decisive factor is that the framework must remain intact even if this or that element should be absent. This is what is new about Group Form, and it seems particulary appropriate to our times.

Significantly, when describing the form, these architects tend to take their analogies from nature. Thus, the redevelopment project of Shiniyuku, one of Tokyo's liveliest districts, is likened to a flower, whose petals, formed by various places of entertainment, are grouped around a central point, the public square. This project will retain its form and function even if one or the other petal is changed or dropped.

The new design for Shintuyu is typical of Metabolist architecture and its possibilities. Three spheres, divided into separate functions, are here loosely connected. A shopping-centre, grouped around the station, an office sector with garages and parking-spaces accessible by pedestrian links, and, on the other side of the station, the entertainment area on which the architects have lavished special attention.

This is how it appears in Maki's and Otaka's description. The entertainment area is shaped like a flower. The square forms the centre from which opera houses, theatres, cinemas, concert and music-halls radiate. The total picture remains even if single petals should be missing. The shopping-centre offers facilities for wholesale and retail buying, eating, drinking and conversation, while in the business section tall tower-like buildings are crowded into a confined space like stars into the Milky Way. Where columns, pillars, arches and other such devices were once used to create a sense of space in the case of single buildings, Group Form uses walls, wells and levels for the construction of our visual environment.

The editors then continue in more general terms: internal and external space is developed simultaneously, and through certain aspects of its design, Group Form will bring into expression a sense of concentrated urban energy.

Here we really are dealing with a new development which cannot be compared with town-planning as we know it. Town-planning used to stand for an essentially static coherence, worked out on paper at the planning-stage. Even so, it could not always be put into practice and foten had to be adapted as the requirements changed during its execution. This concept is due for a shake-up. It must be reorganized and made more flexible. Plans must correspond to the living process of social development, and, as has already been said, it is not a question of isolated buildings but of planning in terms of a living coherent whole. These new ideas, long since recognized in Europe and America as theoretically feasible (it is decades since Mondrian first spoke of the end of singularity in form, and the beginnings of the culture of conscious relationships), are fought for in Japan with conviction so **28** radical that it should help to pave the way to their realization.

KIYONORI KIKUTAKE

Kiyonori Kikutake, of the original Metabolist group, is one of the most influential young Japanese architects. He can look back on considerable achievements. Born in 1928, he began his studies at Waseda University in Tokyo. His first success came when he won the third prize for his design of the church in the Peace Centre of Hiroshima in a competition. (First prize not awarded: second prize, Kenzo Tange.) Doubtless due to the influence of his striking work, the students of Waseda won three prizes at the São Paolo Biennale while Kikutake was at the University. After finishing his studies, he first worked in the firm of Takenaka, then with Marano and Muri, and later with Motowo Tawe's research team at Waseda.

In 1953, when he was twenty-five, Kikutake opened his own office. Since then, he has been responsible for such important building schemes as the highrise block of flats for employees of the Bridgestone Tyre Company in the Kanagawa prefecture, blocks of flats and detached houses, a cultural centre in Kurume on Kyushu, the Narimasu Mental Hospital in Tokyo (plates 104–105), the museum of the Shimane prefecture (plates 70–71), and his own combined house and office (plates 162–165.) In recent years have followed the City Hall in Tatabayashi (plates 26–27), the gymnasia of Hitotsubashi Junior High School and his most important work, the great shrine at Izumo. Here Kikutake presented an entirely new concept of Shintoist religious architecture, applying Metabolist flexibility to the age-old custom of refurbishing shrine-architecture every twenty years. He said of this building, completed in 1964, that we must stop thinking in terms of form and function and instead begin to think in terms of space and variable functions. This is why the *kata* of Metabolist architecture is defined as harmony of space and useful function.

In old Japanese, *kata* used in this connection means the technical side of architecture. Kikutake incorporated this into his three-tier methodology. It begins with the concept *ka,* meaning the image, the idea. In combination with the technical aspects, it leads to *katachi,* the building's function.

Kikutake's endeavours towards the creation of a new urban order according to Metabolist principles started as early as 1958. In January 1959, the Japanese journal *Kokosai Kenchiku* published his scheme for a tower-city. In the February issue of the same publication followed the plan for a city floating on the sea on gigantic concrete rafts, below which residential blocks are suspended into the sea. Both these projects (plates 172–173), visionary yet practical and future-orientated, were subsequently combined in the project 'Unabara'.

The designs are at the same time urbanist and architectural, it is no longer possible to make a distinction. In the explanation of his tower-city, Kikutake went into the question of contemporary urban planning with special reference to Tokyo. For him town-planning must not ignore the state of affairs of today. We were moving towards the height of chaos. Urban planning must bring a new hope to our cities which had lost all sense of direction and whose harmony has been destroyed.

At the same time, Kikutake is not uncritical of his project, which he really regards as a theoretical concept to be put into practice only with modifications.

He sees in it the same basic idea which is echoed in other Metabolist projects; attention paid to it would remove many misunderstandings.

Kikutake's ocean-city contains his suggestions for a maritime urban civilization. Communal activities are intended to take place on islands which are, for the most part, artificially created and float on the water's surface. The residential blocks hang into the water. They are surrounded by the sea on the outside and ventilated by means of wide internal shafts, open at the top. The ancient Japanese predilection for water has here been given expression in modern terms.

Kikutake ends his explanation by stating that since the ocean-city is artificially created, each special function must be planned for in the basic scheme, which is dedicated to the new maritime society and promises men a new future.

Kikutake's reminder that 70 % of the earth's surface is covered by water, and the fact that the envisaged maritime society would require that there be no danger of war because of its extreme vulnerability, give this project a significance the implications of which extend far beyond the sphere of architecture.

As has been said, 'unabara' is the combination of two previously separate schemes. It is intended for a population of roughly half a million and planned east of the Bay of Tokyo in Sagami Bay. The author describes the plan as a project for a city consisting of two rings: an inner residential ring and an outer, industrial one. They are linked by an administration block.

The city's centre would be inhabited; it was essential that men should live in the centres of any future cities.

Thus Kikutake's importance lies not only in his various buildings, but even more especially in the projects outlined above, which will be decisive for the development of architecture. In addition, Kikutake has worked on detailed projects for the industrialization of the building trade. His adaptable detached house, for instance, plays a great part in his urban proposals. He divides the elements of this house into flexible separate cells consisting of kitchen, bathroom, nursery and living-room units. Different units can then be assembled into family-apartments. The large Mova block (plate 180) consists of many of these adaptable cells, and the large blocks form the urban entity. Not enough attention has yet been paid to Kikutake's research. It will undoubtedly play an important part in the urban projects should they ever be realized. In principle, the whole and its parts are constructed in accordance with the same rules and so condition each other.

YOSHITAKE AKUI

Not only the Metabolists, but other groups of young Japanese architects are occupied with work on superstructures. Yoshitake Akui (born in 1930) and Taizo Nozawa (born 1934) have, in collaboration, produced designs comparable to those of the Metabolists. They also foresee fundamental changes in our entire social situation.

Akui studied landscape architecture at Tokyo University and worked from 1956–1963 in the offices of Kenzo Tange, mostly on the designs for Tokyo Cathedral. From 1963–1965 he had his own offices and then went to Europe where he first worked in Zurich and then in Berlin, successfully taking part in urban design competitions (Düsseldorf-Ratingen).

His proposals for the reform of the urban organism date mainly from 1964. His superstructures, called Neo Mastaba (plate 176), are models for new urban bodies which, suspended above ground and supported by struts, are arranged in tiers. These are in every case to be adjusted to individual sociological, local and architectural conditions. According to Akui, 25.000 to 30.000 people could live and work in each of these urban units, and form a self-contained organism.

Akui and his collaborator Nozowa are sure that it would be far from impractical to erect such enormous city-structures, which bear a similarity to the pyramids and the buildings in ancient China. These monuments, still admired today, were erected by despotic methods and the most primitive means, and technically conditions now are incomparably better. All that would be needed today is the co-ordination of the various existing facilities.

Akui, also, starts from the premise that the conditions of life in our society must be given appropriately dynamic buildings, so that flexible structures, adjustable to varying demands, become a necessity. He too, like other architects of his generation, tends to use biological metaphors to explain his projects.

Akui sees the new urban structure as a chain of his large, pyramid-shaped Neo Mastabas linked by traffic-bands and thus permanently capable of change and growth. The result of Akui's proposals, however, would be a new rhythm in men's lives. The seven-day week, with its fixed days of work and rest, which has changed in the course of the last few years in any case, would possibly have to give way to a division of time more favourable to the better organization of the vital rhythm of society.

ARATA ISOZAKI

Arata Isozaki was not a founder-member of the Metabolist group but joined it, together with his teacher Kenzo Tange, in 1964. Born in Oita on the island of Kiushu, Isotaki took his architectural diploma in Tokyo in 1954. For the next seven years he worked in the offices of Kenzo Tange. From the start, he was chiefly occupied with urban projects. In 1962 he opened his own offices in Tokyo. Amongst his completed buildings are a high school (plates 66–67) at Oita (1964), the central library (plates 62–63) in Oita (1964–66) and a block of flats in Tokyo (1964) distinguished by their powerful structure and the imaginative way in which rough concrete has been used. Isozaki also participated in such international competitions as the one for the Peugeot building in Buenos Aires.

His urban projects have a very direct actuality. They express the new radical intent of the young Japanese architects. When Isozaki was collaborating with Kenzo Tange on the plan for Tokyo in 1960, he was already using his off-the-ground bridge-spanning methods for one of the areas (plate 179). He created powerful living units, supported by masts of various heights. Ties with old Japanese traditions are also in this case neither extraneous nor accidental. The construction of the massive, old Japanese wooden temples or pagodas bears an astonishing resemblence to these differently dimensioned residential towns. In 1962 Isozaki created visionary designs (plate 178) for aerial dwellings, huge living-storeys jutting out from central masts, which recall the wooden Japanese architecture of the seventh and eighth century. The architect of the technological era has rediscovered in them a vitality already attained thousands of years ago.

Past, present and future have rearranged themselves on a new spiritual plane for the young architects, more so even than they had for Mayekawa and Tange, and this has illuminated the achievements of the past as much as the projects of the present.

NORIAKI KUROKAWA

Noriaki Kurokawa, born in Nagoya in 1934, is a founder-member of the Metabolist group. He first studied at Kyoto and took his master's degree in architecture in Tokyo. He then worked in Kenzo Tange's office for several years. In 1960 he, like Arata Isozaki, collaborated on Tange's Tokyo plan. He opened his own office in 1961.

By 1959 he had already attracted attention with his urban schemes and analyses. His proposals for the redevelopment of Tokyo are based on the organic principles of the bamboo plant.

He deliberately planned gigantic vertical constructions in imitation of bamboo, and divided them into zones with horizontal circulation. The base of this city is planned to stand thirty-one metres off the ground, the maximum building-height permitted in Japan in 1959.

Kurokawa also attracted much notice with his Wall-City of 1959. This was published in the Metabolist manifesto of 1960 and appeared as the last feature, so to speak of the magnum opus. Here, Kurokawa is endeavouring to extend the ideas first used by Le Corbusier in his Unité d'Habitation. Kurokawa, however, does not confine himself to single buildings but tackles the urban structure as a whole. He believes that people will be at leisure for three or four days of the week in the not too distant future, and comes to the following conclusion: 'The use of atomic energy will make an extremely dense service system possible, and the division of living space into fixed and mobile units will characterize life in the atomic age.'

Kurokawa sees the city as a gigantic architectural entity, almost as one building, containing housing- as well as working-spheres. He envisages mobile housing-cells which families will be able to move at will to different places for their three or four workfree days. The permanent house incorporated into the basic structure of the urban framework can be completed or extended by these mobile units, which must therefore be more than vehicular in character.

In 1960, Kurokawa developed his Agrar-city, where he tried to surmount the differences between village and city, as in his opinion 'rural communities are townships whose production-methods are agricultural.' He believes that the sum total of men's amenities is made up of agrarian, industrial, consumer and recreational cities. His Agrar-city is based on the 500×500 metre system, already in evidence in old Japanese architecture. This area is to be vertically organized into levels for working, social activity and private life, each with its appropriate architectural expression.

In the years that followed, Kurokawa also occupied himself with mass-housing, and designed and built a number of houses in Tokyo as well as factories in Sagae and Tokyo. He erected several buildings for the 'National Children's Land' in Yokohama (the Hans Christian Andersen house and shelters for children), a hotel in Honjima, and the Nishijin Trade Union Hall in Kyoto (plates 84–85).

New buildings by Kurokawa include the city-hall of Sagae, and the recreation-centres in the Aichi and Yamagata prefectures. He also participated in international competitions such as for the University building in Dublin (1963), Naniwa University (1964), the international congress-hall in Kyoto (1964) and the Allegheny Square in Pittsburgh, USA.

In 1961, Kurokawa published his Helix City Project (plate 177), the development of new designs for a metropolitan superstructure. He was working towards a synthesis of house and street-architecture, an entirely new concept. He considers that Helix must be linked with this 'street-architecture', and is simultaneously a city of movement, which creates a three-dimensional, organic vertical area.

The new perspectives opened up by the projects of this young architect are designed to offer practical solutions to the problems that face us and endeavour to take into account the development of society in cities like Tokyo, New York, Shanghai, and Los Angeles.

NOBORU KAWAZOE

Noboru Kawazoe (born 1926), a critic of architecture who has belonged to the Metabolist group since its beginnings, read architecture and psychology at Waseda University, Tokyo. In Zodiac 9 he wrote that the cities of the future would, whether we liked it or not, far surpass all human standards of scale. They would contain, for example, mammoth buildings, super-blocks and racing-speed motorways. Surrounded by the super-human excess of the three S's: – size, speed and the spirit that would inevitably grow out these two – something would have to be done to relate man to his environment.

In the designs and plans of the Metabolists, Kawazoe sees the possibilities of creating harmony between men and their surroundings. He is convinced that the use of the most highly developed technical and structural means will, ultimately, lead to a new, closer contact with nature.

The crux of the matter is the communication between human activities and organic, natural processes. Kawazoe goes on to say that cities of the future must be capable of controlling the dynamic evolution of nature by technical means. They must be able to hold their own beside dramatic natural features – mountains, lakes, plains and oceans, with rain-storms, typhoons, high tides and volcanoes. Future cities would incorporate nature on the grand scale, as well as on the more human one of trees and rivers.

Furthermore, private dwellings must have a visible individuality. Where a city can be metabolized, it will then be able to contain a variety of buildings without losing its order.

In another place he emphasizes the point that Metabolists relate the word 'Metabolism' not only to the process taking place in each separate living unit, but use it for the concept of continuous renewal which includes all nature – animals and plants, living organisms, natural surroundings, topography, climate and men, as well as the natural forces which give impetus to this all-embracing, high-powered process.

Contemporary architecture has been decisively enriched in its development by the projects and works of the young Japanese architects. Here is the manifestation – for the time being only in visionary terms – of the basic concept that architectural activity can no longer relate to single buildings. The creative design of the new organic cell metropolis will, in coming decades, be based on the initial pioneering of the young Japanese. As Oscar Wilde said in 1891: 'Progress means putting Utopia into practice.'

The Plates

Kenzo Tange: Tokyo City Hall (1952–1957). Administration building.
Below: detail

2 Kenzo Tange: Shimizu City Hall (1953–1954)

Kenzo Tange: Shimizu City Hall. Ground floor entrance hall

4 Kenzo Tange: Kurayoshi City Hall (1955–1956)

Kenzo Tange: Kurayoshi City Hall. Balcony

6 Kenzo Tange: Imabari City Hall (1957–1959). Entrance hall

Kenzo Tange: Imabari City Hall

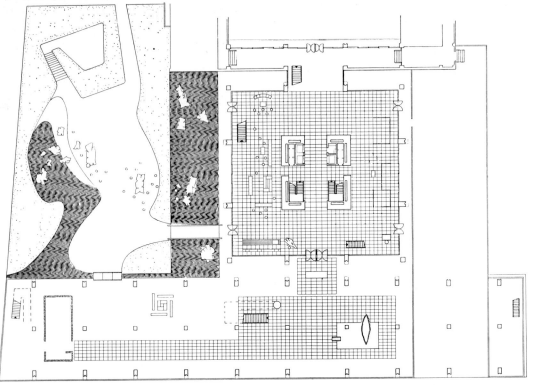

Kenzo Tange: Kagawa Prefecture Government Office,
Takamatsu (1955–1958). General view, site plan
8 Right: Inner court

Kenzo Tange: Kagawa Prefecture Government Office.
10 Pool with rocks in inner court

Kenzo Tange: Kagawa Prefecture Government Office.
Exterior staircase, detail

Kenzo Tange: Kagawa Prefecture Government Office. Lecture hall

Kenzo Tange: Kagawa Prefecture Government Office. Assembly hall **13**

14 Kenzo Tange: Kurashiki City Hall (1958–1960)

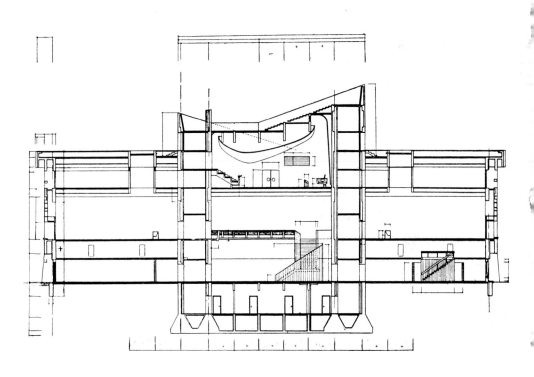

Kenzo Tange: Kurashiki City Hall. Above: general view.
Below: section

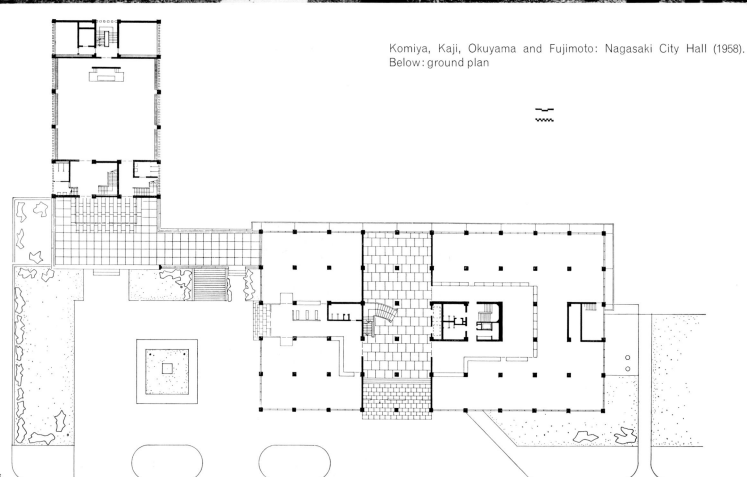

Komiya, Kaji, Okuyama and Fujimoto: Nagasaki City Hall (1958).
Below: ground plan

Komiya, Kaji, Okuyama and Fujimoto: Nagasaki City Hall.
General view in relation to environment

Komiya, Kaji, Okuyama and Fujimoto: Nagasaki City Hall.
18　Entrance to auditorium

Komiya, Kaji, Okuyama and Fujimoto: Nagasaki City Hall.
Terrace and steps

Junzo Sakakura: Hajima City Hall

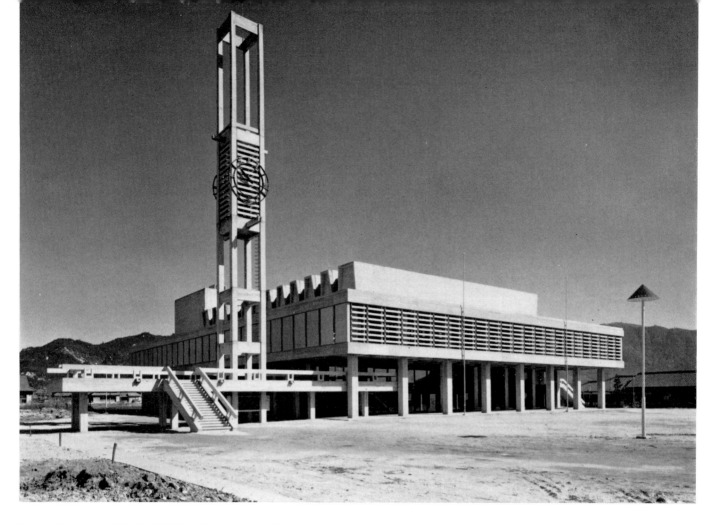

Takeo Sato: Hofu City Hall (1960). Above: general view.
Below: auditorium

Takeo Sato: Iwakuni City Hall (1959). Above: general view.
Below: assembly hall

Japanese Government, Ministry of Construction (the office for the
Kingi province): Nara, Administrative Building of the Nara Prefecture.
Above: view from the air. Below: general view

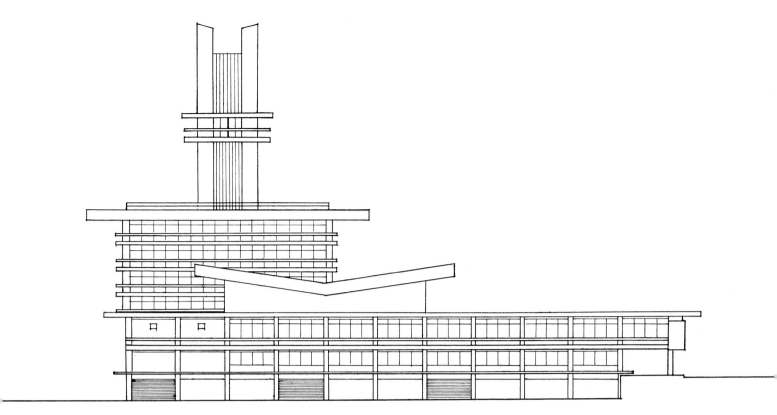

Japanese Government, Ministry of Construction (the office for the Kingi province):
Nara, Administrative Building of the Nara Prefecture.
Above: elevation. Below: inner courtyard

Kiyonori Kikutake: Tatabayashi City Hall (1964). General view

Kiyonori Kikutake: Tatabayashi City Hall. Conference room

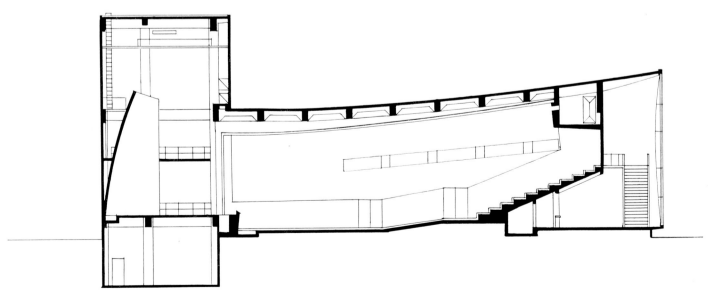

Fuminaga Kiyota: Public Hall, Nakao, Tokyo (1958).
28 Above: façade. Below: section

Togo Murano and Tiuchi Mori: Public Hall, Yonaga (1960). Façade   **29**

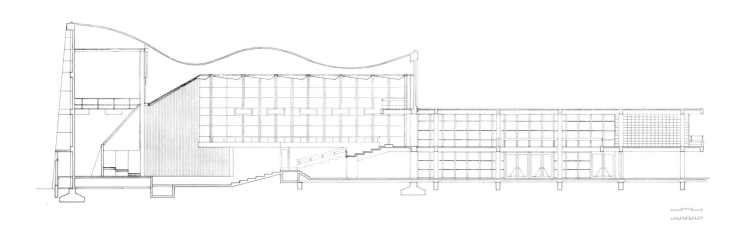

Kunio Mayekawa: Fukushima Educational Centre (1954).
Above: general view. Below: section

Kunio Mayekawa: Fukushima Educational Centre.
Auditorium, looking towards the stage

Kunio Mayekawa: Fukushima Educational Centre.
32　Auditorium, detail of interior

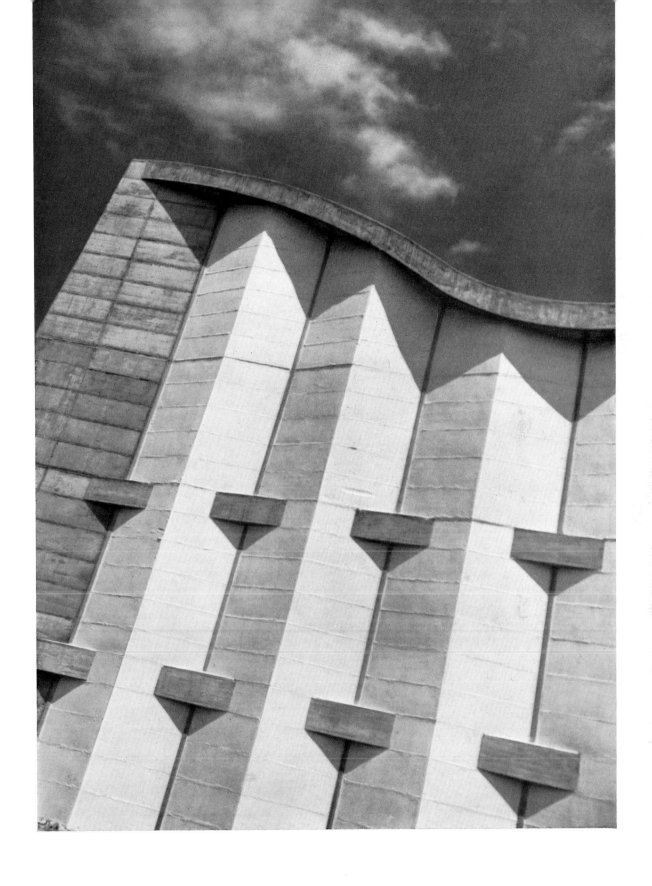

Kunio Mayekawa: Fukushima Educational Centre.
Auditorium, detail of exterior

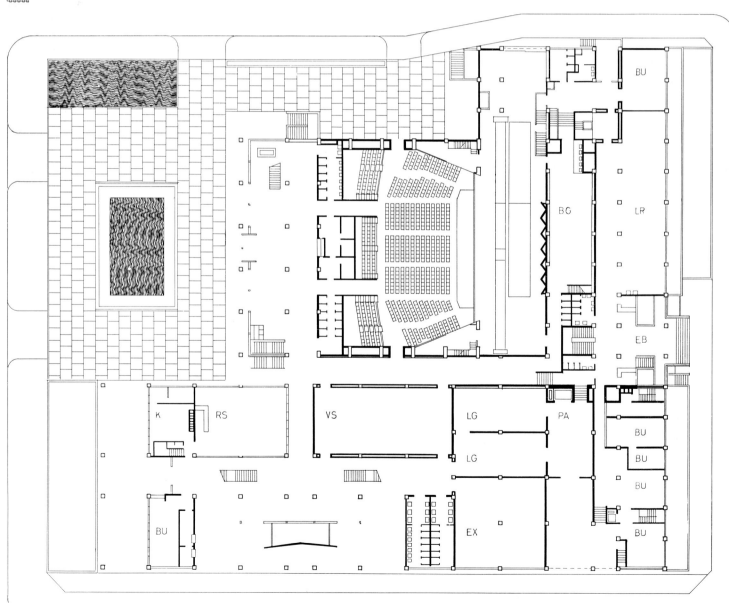

Hideo Kosaka: Aichi Cultural Centre, Nagoya (1959).
Left: general view and ground plan. Above: auditorium building

Kunio Mayekawa: Tokyo, Setagaya Cultural Centre (1958).

Auditorium, detail of exterior

Kunio Mayekawa: Tokyo, Setagaya Cultural Centre. General view **37**

Kenzo Tange: Ehime Convention Hall at Matsuyama (1952–1953).
Above: general view. Below: ground plan

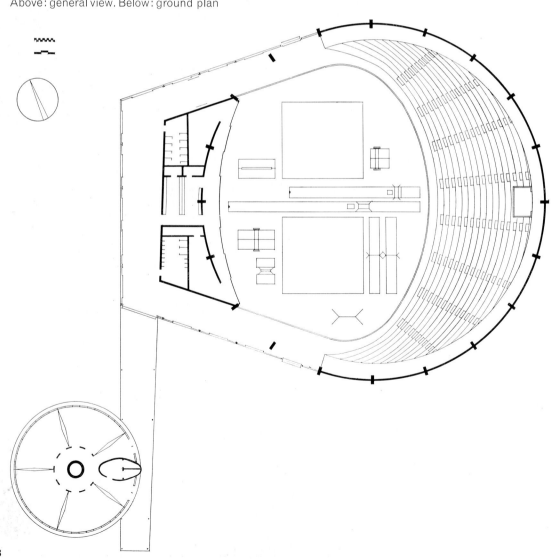

Kenzo Tange: Nichinan Cultural Centre (1963).
Above: general view. Below: model

Right: Kenzo Tange: Nichinan Cultural Centre.
Detail of wall

Junzo Sakakura: Kure Municipal Office and Civic Auditorium. (1962).

Junzo Sakakura: Kure Municipal Office and Civic Auditorium.
Above: interior of the auditorium. Below: municipal office and
congress hall, west elevation

Left: Kunio Mayekawa: Okayama Cultural Centre (1962)

Kunio Mayekawa: Tokyo Cultural Centre (1960). Tokyo Metropolitan Festival Hall.
Above: general view. Below: view from the air

Kunio Mayekawa: Tokyo Cultural Centre. Small Hall

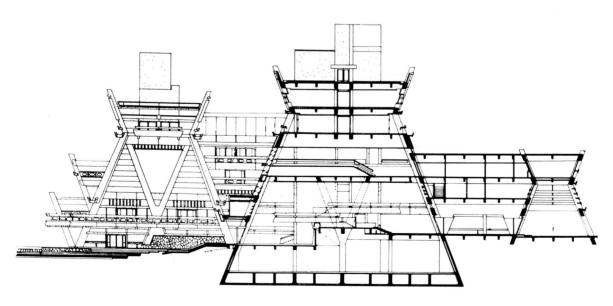

Sachio Ohtani: Kyoto, International Conference Hall (1965).
Above: general view. Below: section

Sachio Ohtani: Kyoto, International Conference Hall. Side elevation

Antonin Raymond and L. L. Rado: Nanzan University in Nagoya.
Above: general view. Below: site plan

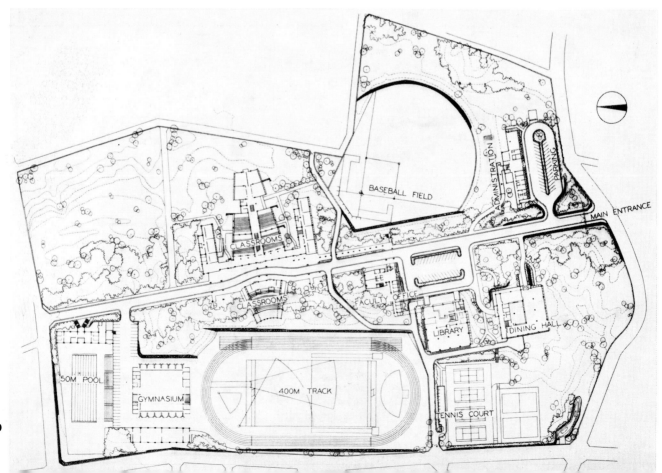

Antonin Raymond and L. L. Rado: Nanzan University in Nagoya.
Above: dining hall, detail. Below: library and office block

Kunio Mayekawa: Tokyo, Gakushuin University (1958)

Right: Tokyo, Gakushuin University Library.
Entrance and forecourt

54 Kenzo Tange: Tsuda College Library, Kodaira, Tokyo (1953–1954)

Kenzo Tange: Tsuda College, Kodaira, Tokyo. Reading room

Kenzo Tange: Tokyo, Rikkyo University. Library.
Reading room on first floor

Left: Kenzo Tange: Tokyo, Rikkyo University (1959–1961). Library

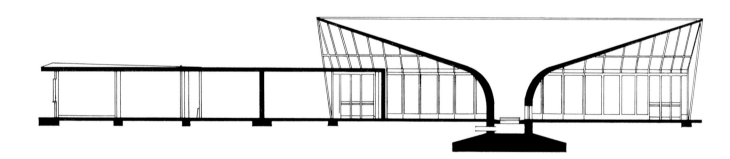

Kenzo Tange: Hiroshima (1951–1952). Children's Library.
Above: view by night. Below: section

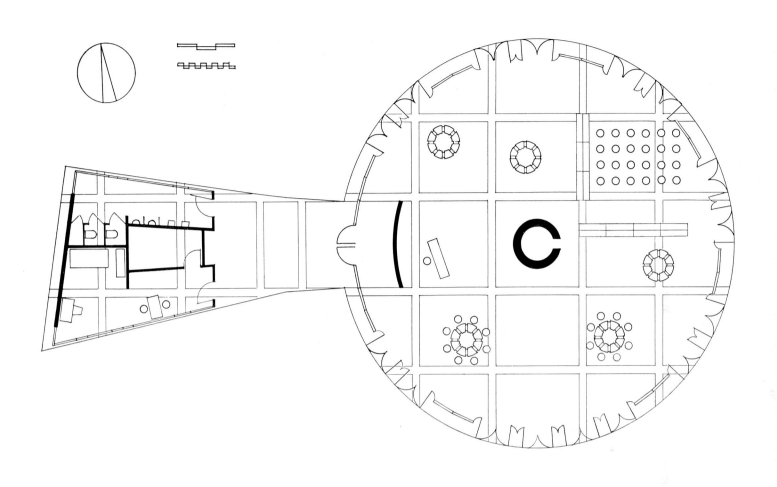

Kenzo Tange: Hiroshima Children's Library. Ground plan

Kenzo Tange: Hiroshima Children's Library. Lecture room

Arata Isozaki: Library at Oita (1966).
Above: general view. Below: entrance

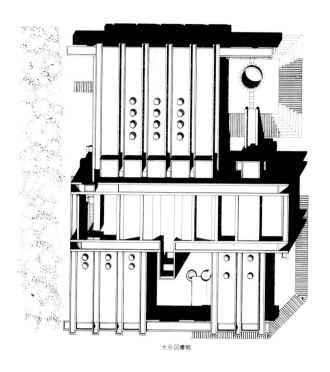

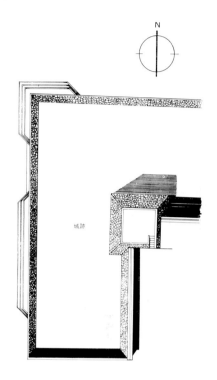

大分図書館

Arata Isozaki: Library at Oita. Above: ground plan. Below: Reading room

Takamasa Yoshizaka: High School in Nagasaki (1958).
64 General view from south

Takamasa Yoshizaka: High School in Nagasaki.
Above: south elevation, detail. Below: north elevation

Arata Isozaki: School at Oita (1964). General view   Right: Arata Isozaki: School at Oita. Detail

Le Corbusier, Junzo Sakakura, Kunio Mayekawa and
Takamasa Yoshizaka:
68   Tokyo, Museum of Modern Art (1959)

Le Corbusier, Junzo Sakakura, Kunio Mayekawa and
Takamasa Yoshizaka:
Tokyo, Museum of Modern Art

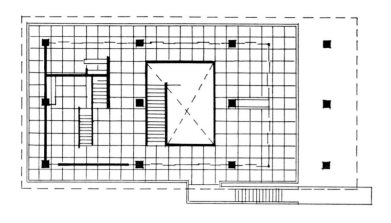

1.0G

Kiyonori Kikutake: Museum and Art Gallery of the Shimane
Prefecture, Matsue (1960).
70 Above: entrance. Below: first floor plan

Kiyonori Kikutake: Museum and Art Gallery of the Shimane
Prefecture, Matsue. Detail

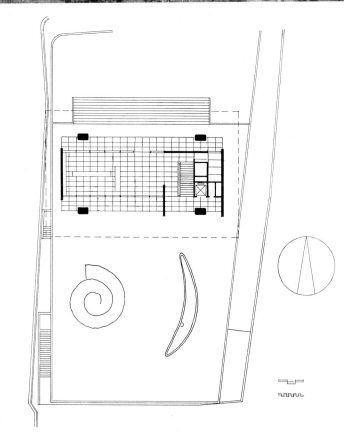

Kenzo Tange: Tokyo, Sogetsu Art Centre (1955–1958).

Right: Kenzo Tange: Tokyo, Sogetsu Art Centre. Main entrance

Above: view from the park. Below: floor plan

Kunio Mayekawa: Yokohama, Kanagawa Library and Concert Hall
74 (1954)

Antonin Raymond and L. L. Rado: Concert Hall in Takasaki (1958–62).
Gumma Music Centre.
76 Above: exterior. Below: façade and entrance

Antonin Raymond and L. L. Rado: Concert Hall in Takasaki.
Gumma Music Centre. The stage in the large hall

Yoshinobu Ashihara: Yokohama, Iwasaki Dressmaking School,
78   Yokohama Ladies' Centre (1957–1961)

Yoshinobu Ashihara: Yokohama, Iwasaki Dressmaking School,
Yokohama Ladies' Centre

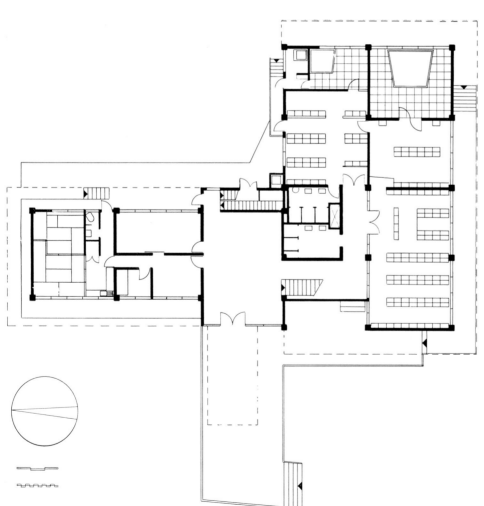

Masachika Murata: Toyu Club House
(1958).
Above: general view. Below: ground plan

Masachika Murata: Aichi Country Club (1958).
Above: general view. Below: ground plan

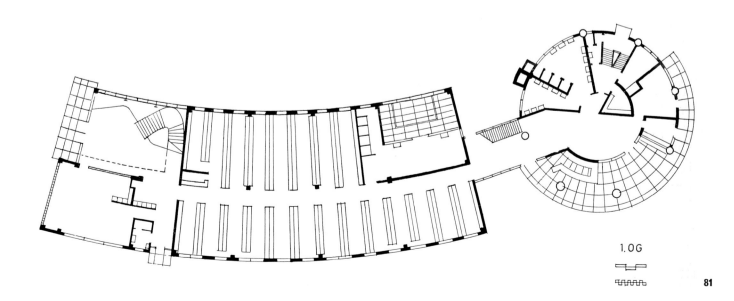

1.0 G

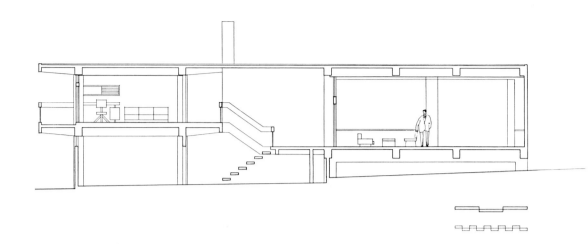

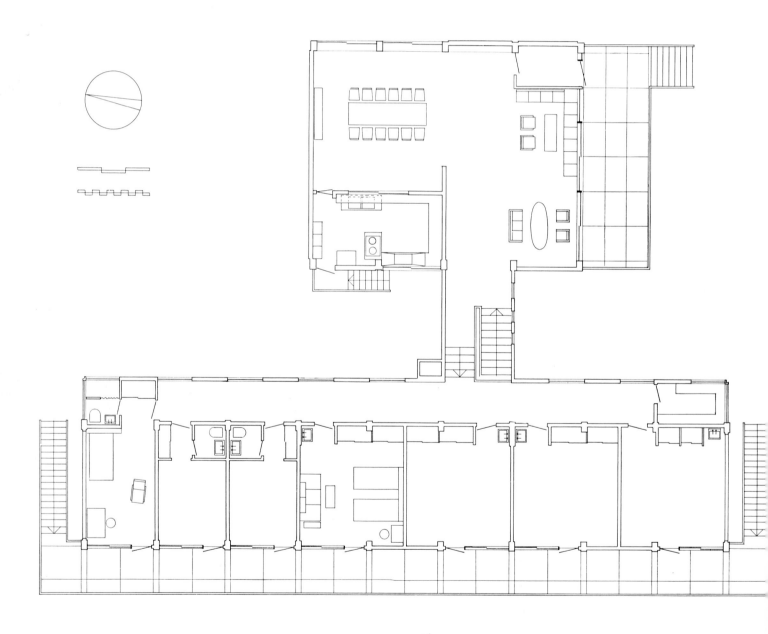

Yoshinobu Ashihara: Matsuhama Club House in Niigata (1956).

82 Above: east-west section. Below: ground plan

Yoshinobu Ashihara: Matsuhama Club House in Niigata.
Above: entrance. Below: side elevation

Left: Noriaki Kurokawa: Kyoto, Nishijn Trade Union Centre (1962)

Above: Nishijn Trade Union Centre. Plan of site

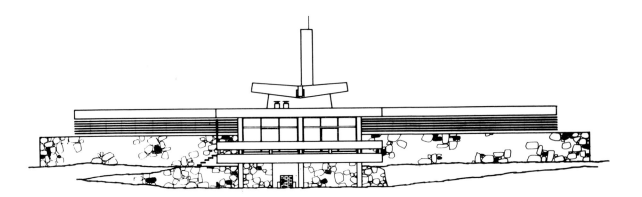

Yoshinobu Ashihara: Youth hostel in Nikko.
Above: south elevation. Below: general view

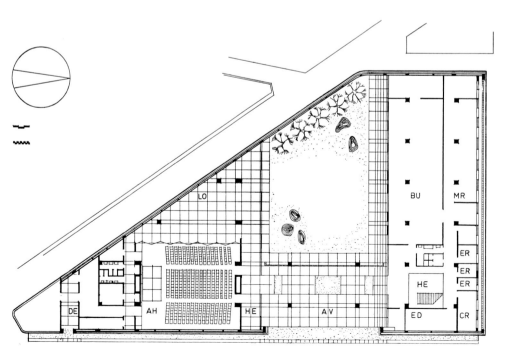

Kenzo Tange: Sumi Memorial
Hall in Ichonomiya (1955–1957).
Above: general view. Below:
88 ground plan

Kenzo Tange: Sumi Memorial Hall in Ichonomiya. Internal court and car-port

Kenzo Tange: Sumi Memorial Hall in Ichonomiya.
Lobby of assembly hall

Kenzo Tange: Golf Club building in Totsuka (1963).
Above: general view. Below: terrace, detail

Kenzo Tange: Golf Club building in Totsuka. Interior

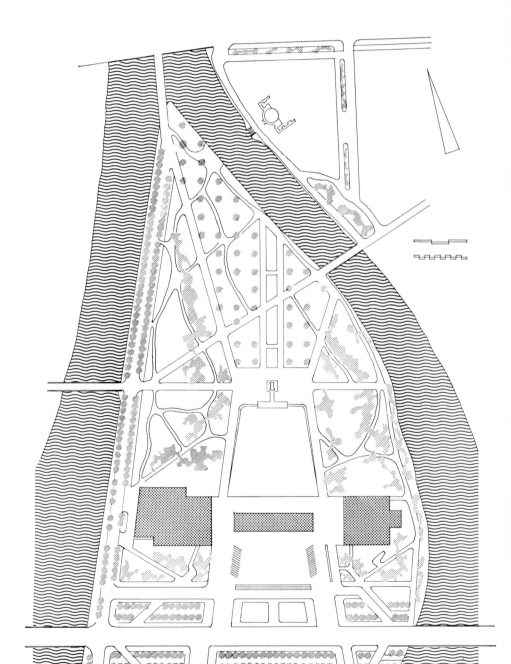

Kenzo Tange: Hiroshima Peace Centre
(1949–1956).
Above: model. Below: site plan

Opposite:
94 Exterior, stepping stones

Kenzo Tange: Hiroshima Peace Centre. Left: Memorial Museum.
Right: Community Centre

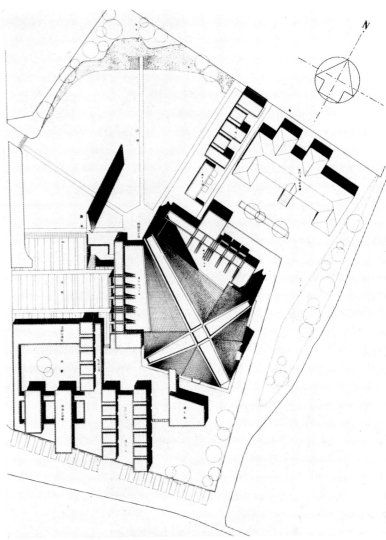

Kenzo Tange: Tokyo Cathedral (1962–1964).
98 Above left: general view of entrance. Above right: site plan

Kenzo Tange: Tokyo Cathedral.
Above: interior.
Below: side elevation

Mamoru Yamada: Tokyo Social Welfare Hospital.
Above: view from the air.
Below: observation lounge

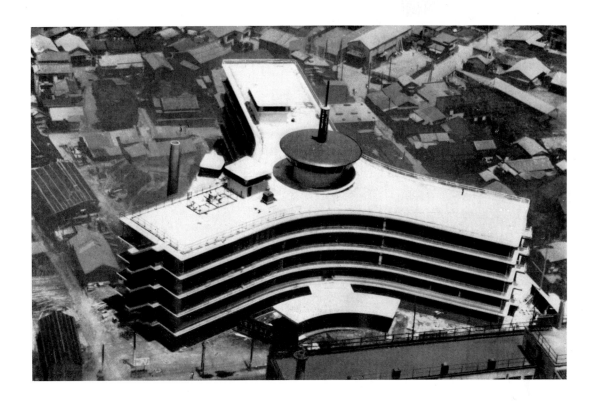

Mamoru Yamada: Tokyo Social Welfare Hospital (1953).
Above: view from the air. Below: ground plan

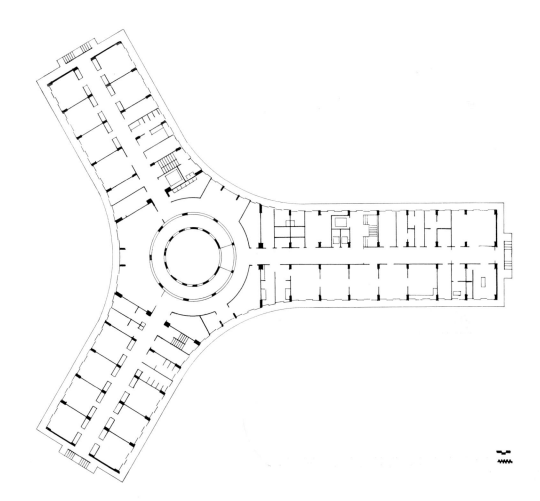

Mamoru Yamada: Osaka University Hospital (1954–1956).

102 Façade and entrance

Mamoru Yamada: Osaka University Hospital. Detail

Kiyonori Kikutake: Tokyo, Narimasu Mental Hospital

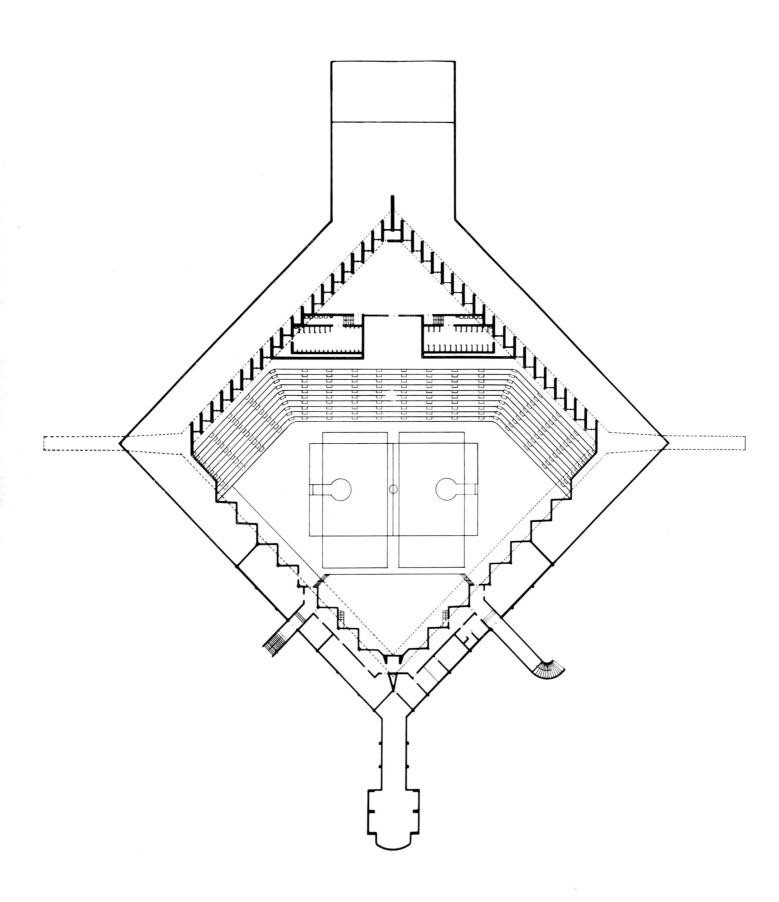

106 Kenzo Tange: Shizuoka Convention Hall (1955–1957). Ground plan

Kenzo Tange: Shizuoka Convention Hall

Eiji Miyagawa, Katsuiti Sezikawa and Hisao Honda: Gymnasium in
Niigata (1959–1960). Above: general view. Below: detail

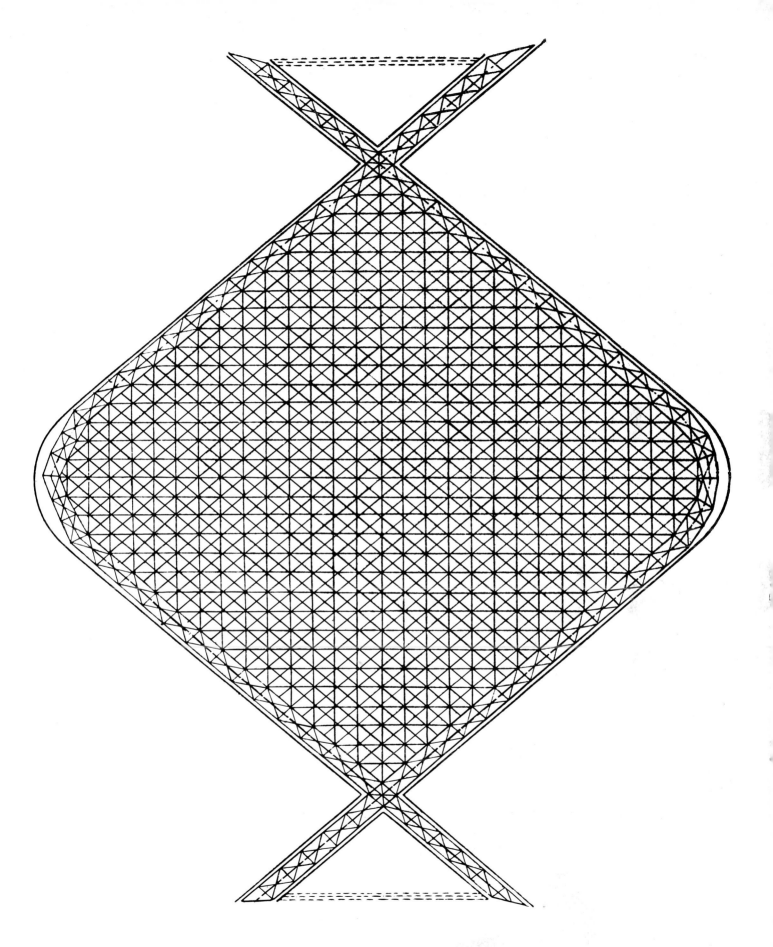

Eiji Miyagawa, Katsuiti Sezikawa and Hisao Honda: Gymnasium in Niigata. Hyperbolic paraboloid shell ceiling plan

Junzo Sakakura: Saga Prefectural Gymnasium, Saga (1963).
110 View from north-west

Junzo Sakakura: Saga Prefectural Gymnasium, Saga. General view **111**

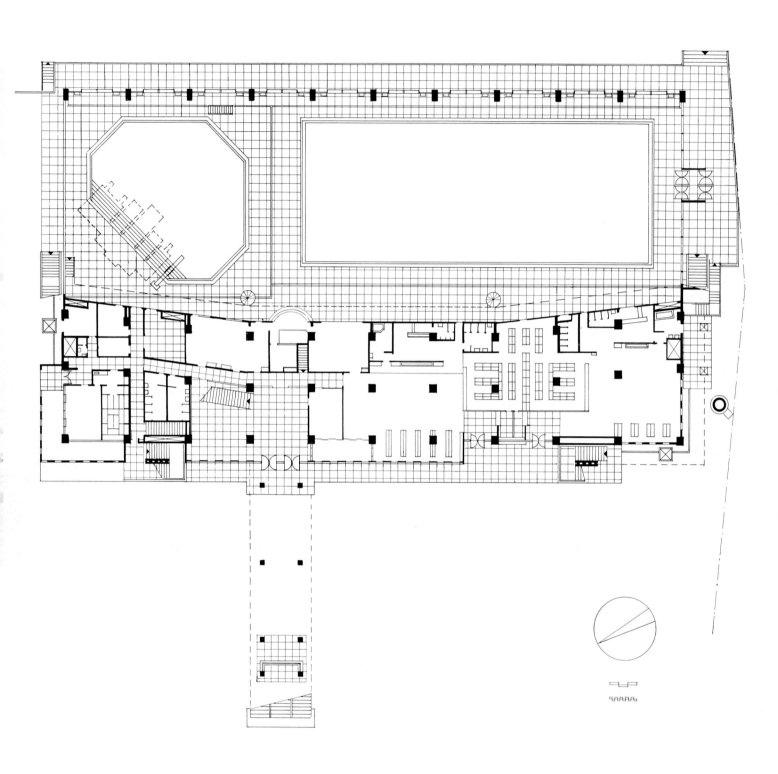

Masachika Murata: Sendagaya Swimming Stadium, Tokyo (1958).
112 Ground plan

Masachika Murata: Sendagaya Swimming Stadium, Tokyo. Entrance **113**

Masachika Murata: Sendagaya Swimming Stadium, Tokyo.
Interior at night

Right: Masachika Murata: Sendagaya Swimming Stadium, Tokyo.
Interior, detail

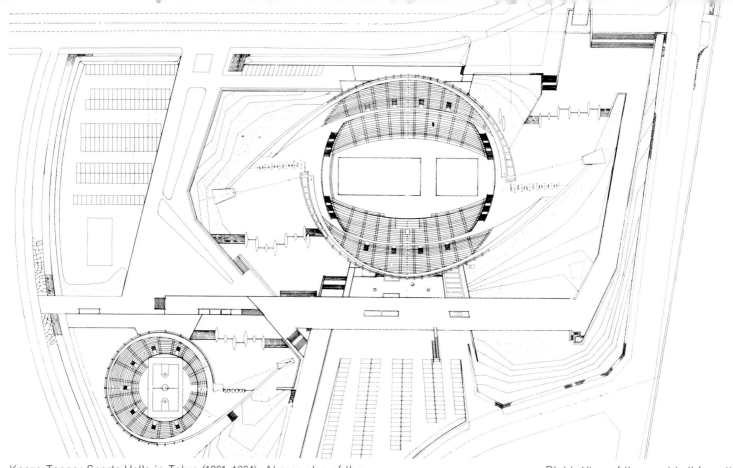

Kenzo Tange: Sports Halls in Tokyo (1961–1964). Above: plan of the
entire complex. Below: view from the south

Right: View of the great hall from the
small hall

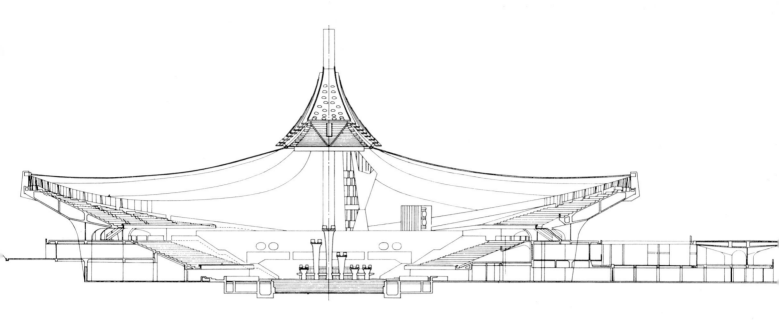

Kenzo Tange: Sports Halls in Tokyo. Olympic Main Stadium.
Above: section. Below: interior

Right: Kenzo Tange: Sports Halls in Tokyo. Olympic Small Stadium
Interior

Kenzo Tange: Hotel in Atami (1962–1963).
120 Above: view from the park. Right: detail

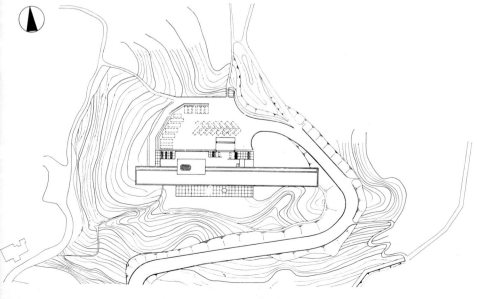

Kiyonori Kikutake: Norioka Grand Hotel,
Norioka (1965)
Above: view by night.
Below: site plan.
Left: general view in relation
to environment

Yoshitaka Akui: Public Hotel Taromachi (1965). Detail.
Left: view from the coast

Isao Shibaoka: Bath-house of a hotel in Kaike, Yonaga (1957).
Above: view from the garden. Below: ground plan

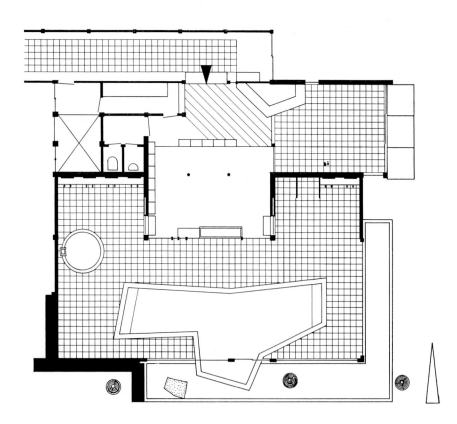

Isao Shibaoka: Bath-house of a hotel in Kaike, Yonaga.
Above: bathroom with view of the garden. Below: bath room seen
from the garden

128 Hideo Kosaka: Kyoto Post Office Savings Bank (1955). Garden elevation

Hideo Kosaka: Kyoto Post Office Savings Bank. Roof terrace

130 Hideo Kosaka: Nagoya Post Office Savings Bank (1959). Side elevation

Hideo Kosaka: Nagoya Post Office Savings Bank. General view

132 Hideo Kosaka: Nagoya Post Office Savings Bank. Hall

Hideo Kosaka: Nagoya Post Office Savings Bank. Rear wall of hall **133**

Toshiro Yamashita: Ogochi Dam Administration building (1958).
Above: balcony. Below: exterior steps

Toshiro Yamashita: Ogochi Dam Administration building.
Above: general view. Below: floor plan

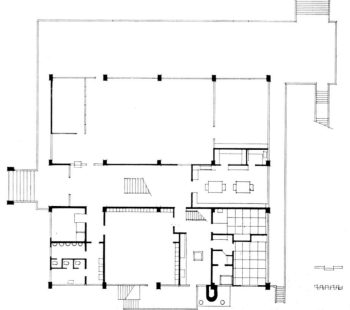

135

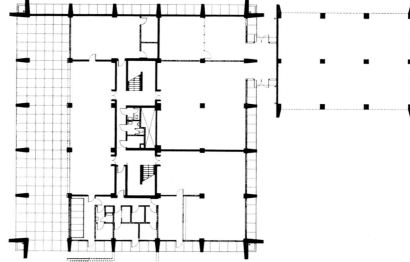

Kiyoshi Kawasaki: Office building in Kobe (1963).
Above: detail
136 Below: plan of ground floor

Kiyoshi Kawasaki: Office building in Kobe. Assembly hall

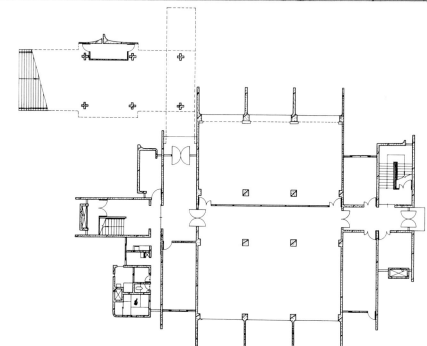

Kiyoshi Kawasaki and Masaru Matsuda: Hiwaka Head
Office Building for Agricultural Co-operative Association.
138 Above: side elevation. Below: plan of ground floor

Kiyoshi Kawasaki and Masaru Matsuda: Hiwaka Head Office Building
for Agricultural Co-operative Association. **139**

Junzo Sakakura: Above: Yokohama, Silk Centre Administration Building (1959). Façade.
Below: Osaka, Laboratory of the Shionogi Pharmaceutical Company. Front elevation

Right: Kenzo Tange: Osaka, Dentsu office building (1957–1960)

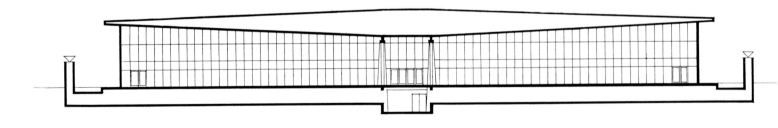

Kenzo Tange: Printing Plant in Numazu (1953–1954).
142 Above: general view. Below: section

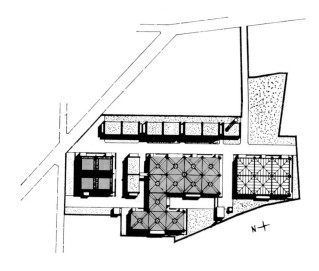

Noriaki Kurokawa: Factory at Sagae, Yamagata (1965).
Above: detail of exterior. Below: ground plan

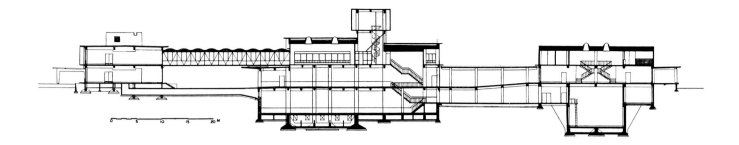

Toshiro Yamashita: Tokyo, Kyodo Milk Plant, Hoya. (1957).
Above: section. Below: view from the air

Toshiro Yamashita: Tokyo, Kyodo Milk Plant, Hoya.
Above: the main factory building to the left, the office wing at the rigth.
Below: bay for delivering goods

146 Yutaro Irie: Spinning mill near Tokyo (1956–1958). View from the air

Yutaro Irie: Spinning mill in Hozumi (1956–1958). View from the air **147**

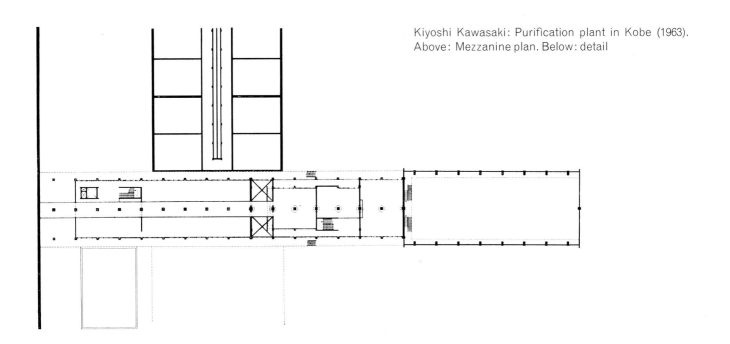

Kiyoshi Kawasaki: Purification plant in Kobe (1963).
Above: Mezzanine plan. Below: detail

Kiyoshi Kawasaki and Gosuke Tobiyama: Otsu Purification Plant (1965). General view

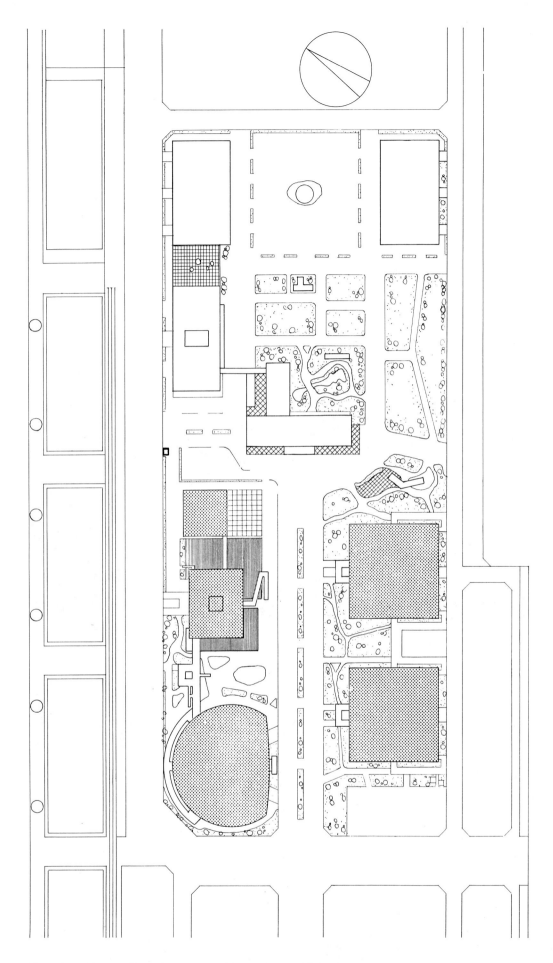

150 Masachika Murata: Tokyo International Trade Centre (1959). Site plan

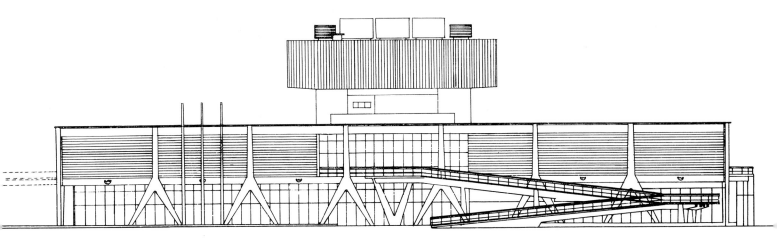

Masachika Murata: Tokyo International Trade Centre.
Above: Hall 3 (front elevation). Below: Hall 1 (entrcane)

Masachika Murata: Tokyo International Trade Centre. Inner court of
Hall 3

Masachika Murata: Tokyo International Trade Centre. Administration
building and refreshment room

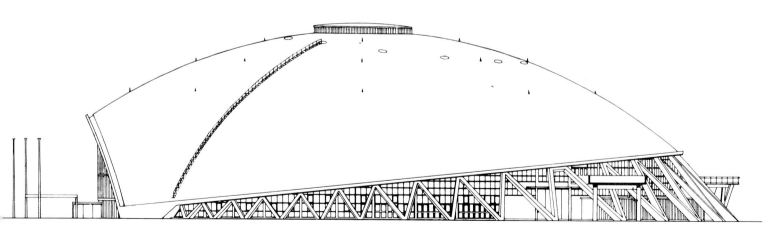

Masachika Murata: Tokyo International Trade Centre.
154 Above: Hall 2, general view. Below: Hall 2 side elevation

Masachika Murata: Tokyo International Trade Centre. Hall 2, interior **155**

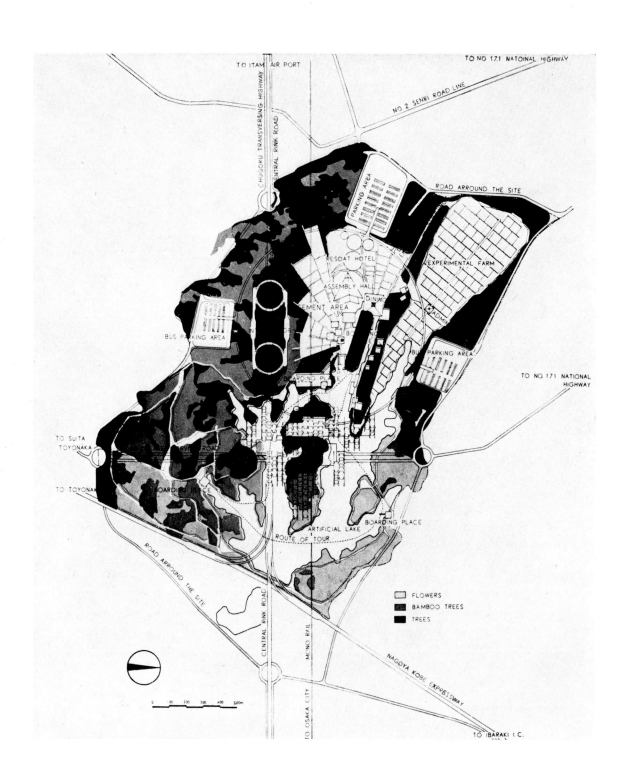

156 Kiyoshi Kawasaki: Project EXPO 70, Osaka (1967). General site plan

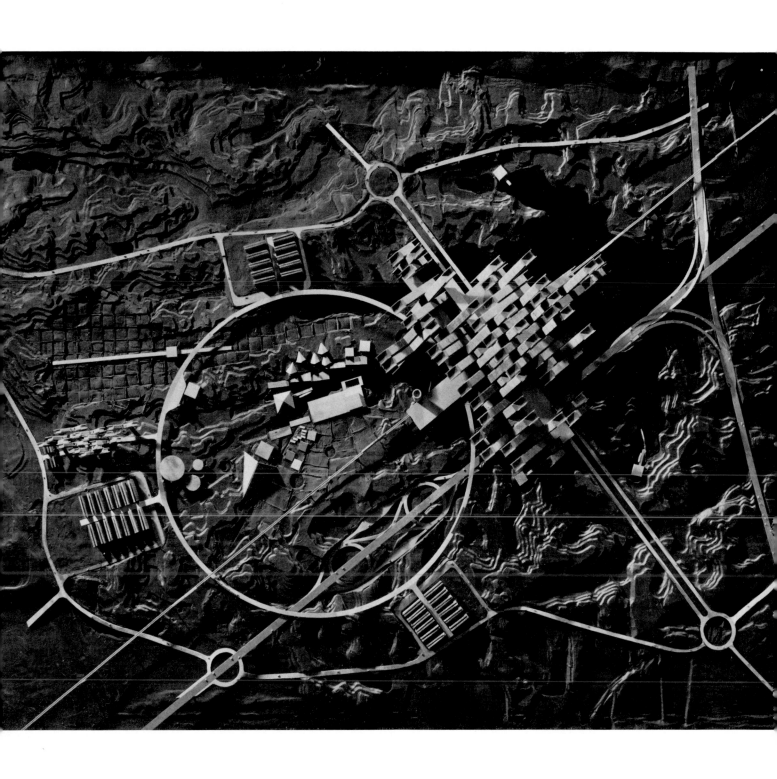

Kiyoshi Kawasaki: Project EXPO 70, Osaka. Model

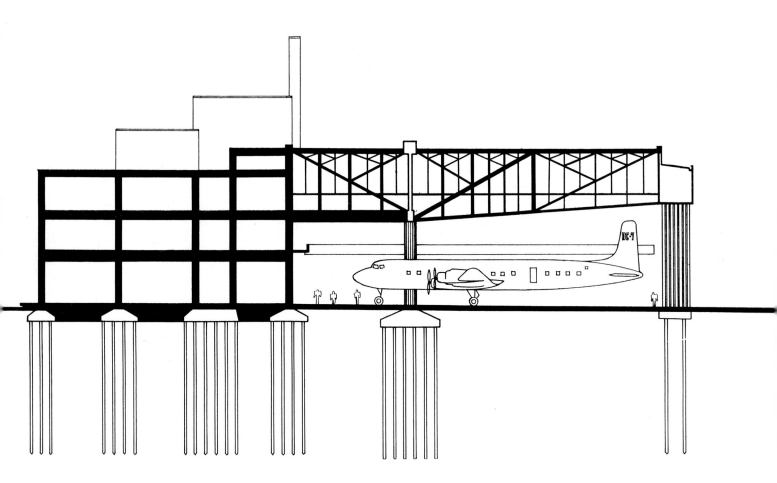

Fuminaga Kiyota: Aircraft hangar in Tokyo (1957).
158 Above: general view. Below: section

Fuminaga Kiyota: Aircraft hangar in Tokyo.
Above: general view. Below: propeller and engine stores

Takamasa Yoshizaka:
Above: Tokyo, Private house (1956). Below: Villa Coucou in Tokyo (1956)

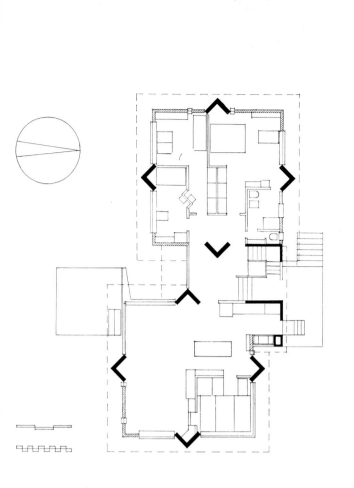

Takamasa Yoshizaka: House in Kobe (1958).
Above left: floor plan. Above right: detail. Below: general view **161**

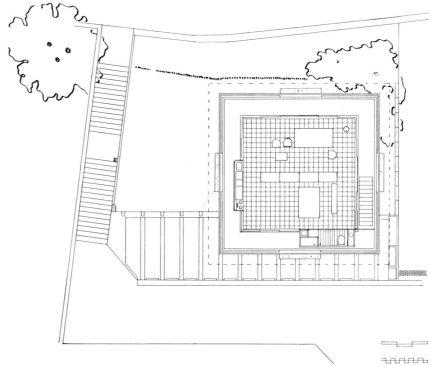

Kiyonari Kikutake: The architect's house in
162 Tokyo (1958).
Above: general view. Below: site plan

Kiyonari Kikutake: The architect's house in Tokyo by night

Kiyonari Kikutake: The architect's house in Tokyo.
Interior with kitchen

Kunio Mayekawa: Tokyo, Harumi Apartment House (1956–1958).

Kunio Mayekawa: Tokyo, Harumi Apartment House. General view **167**

Kiyonori Kikutake: Apartment House in Tonogaya near Yokohama
(1957). General view

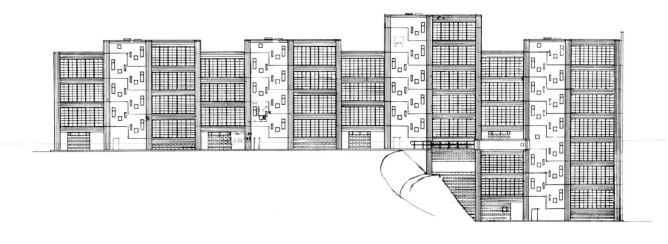

Kiyonari Kikutake: Apartment house in Tonogaya near Yokohama.
Above: elevation. Below: view by night

The Japan Housing Corporation:
Above: Tamadaira Housing development, Tokyo. Below: Housing
development in Akabanedei, Tokyo

The Japan Housing Corporation:
Above: Housing development in Takanedei, Prefecture of Chiba.
Below: Housing development in Soka-Matsubara, Prefecture of Saitama **171**

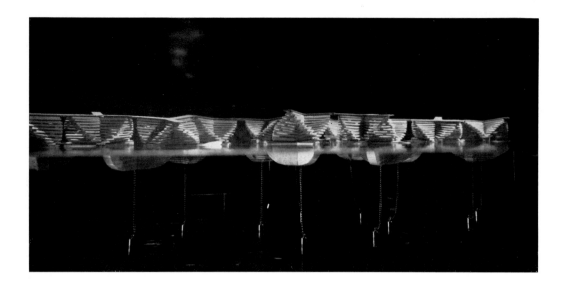

Above: Noriaki Kurokawa: Project for a city on water (1961)
172 Below: Kiyonari Kikutake: Project for a city of towers (1959)

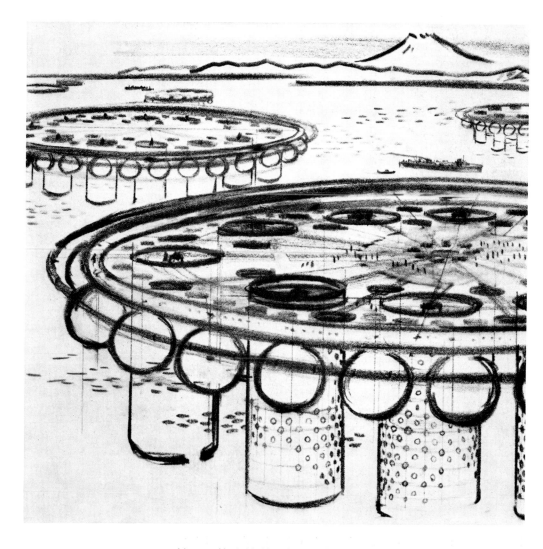

Above: Noriaki Kurokawa: Project for an Agricultural City (1959)
Below: Kiyonari Kikutake: Project for a Marine City (1959)

Kenzo Tange: Project to enlarge Tokyo by extending the city into the
bay of Tokyo.
Above: residential quarter. Below: detail of terraced apartments

Kenzo Tange: Project to enlarge Tokyo. General plan

Yoshitake Akui and Taizo Nozawa: Neo-Mastaba (1964).
Above: model. Below: plan of the region based on Neo-Mastaba

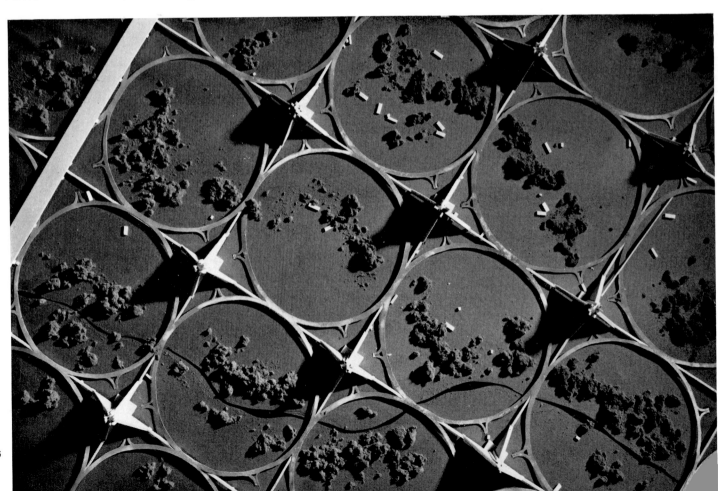

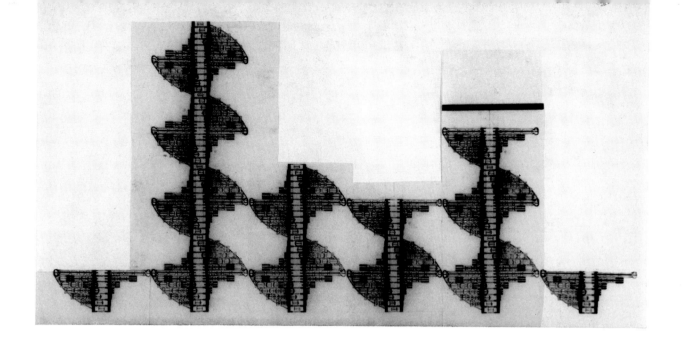

Noriaki Kurokawa: Project for a town (Helix) (1961).
Above: Helix Structure, section. Below: model for a town (1966)

178 Arata Isozaki: Project for a city in the sky. (1962). Model

Arata Isozaki: Project for a centre in Tokyo (1960)

180 Kiyonari Kikutake: Perspective of Mova-Block Constructions (1960)